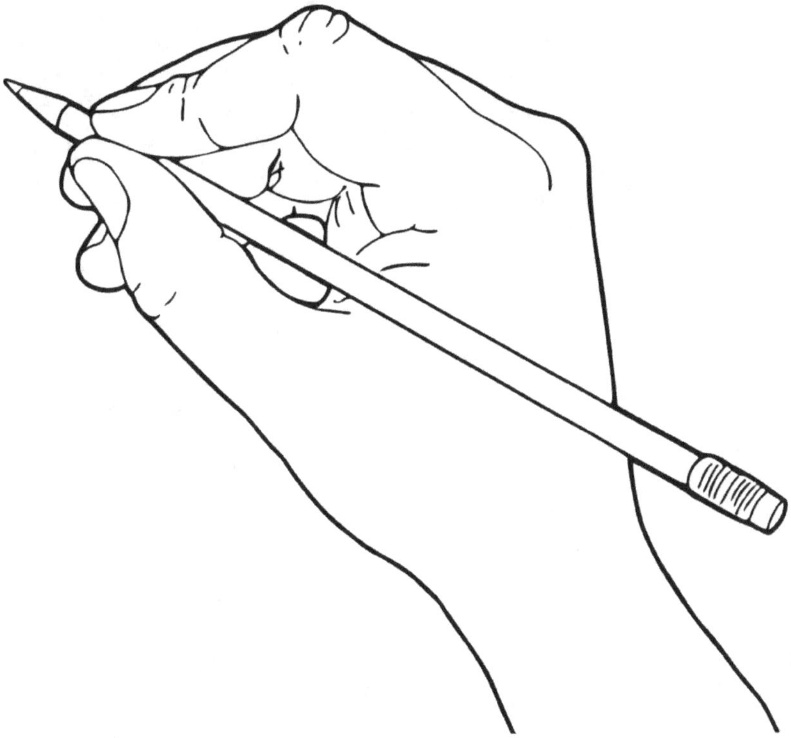

This Notebook belongs to:

____

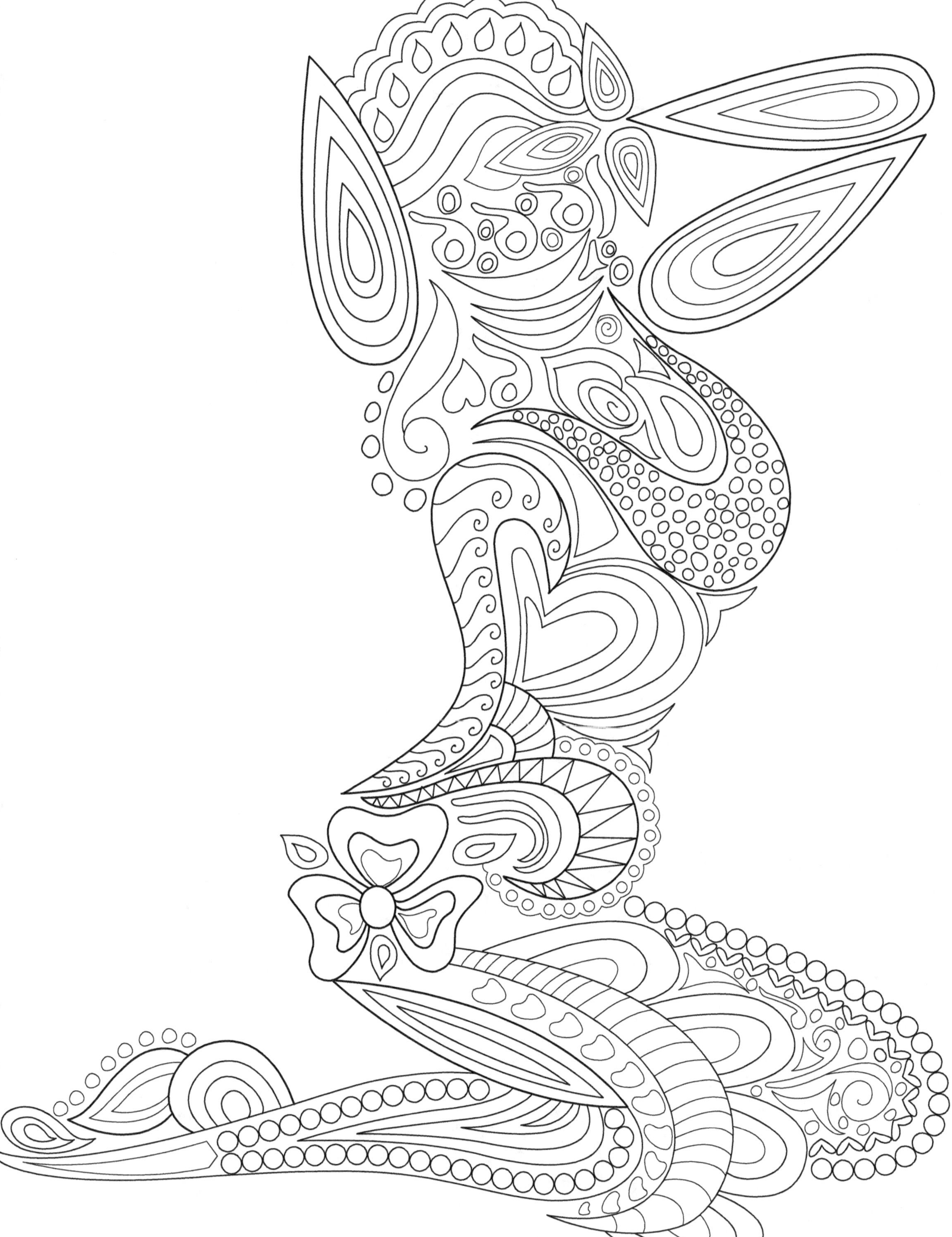

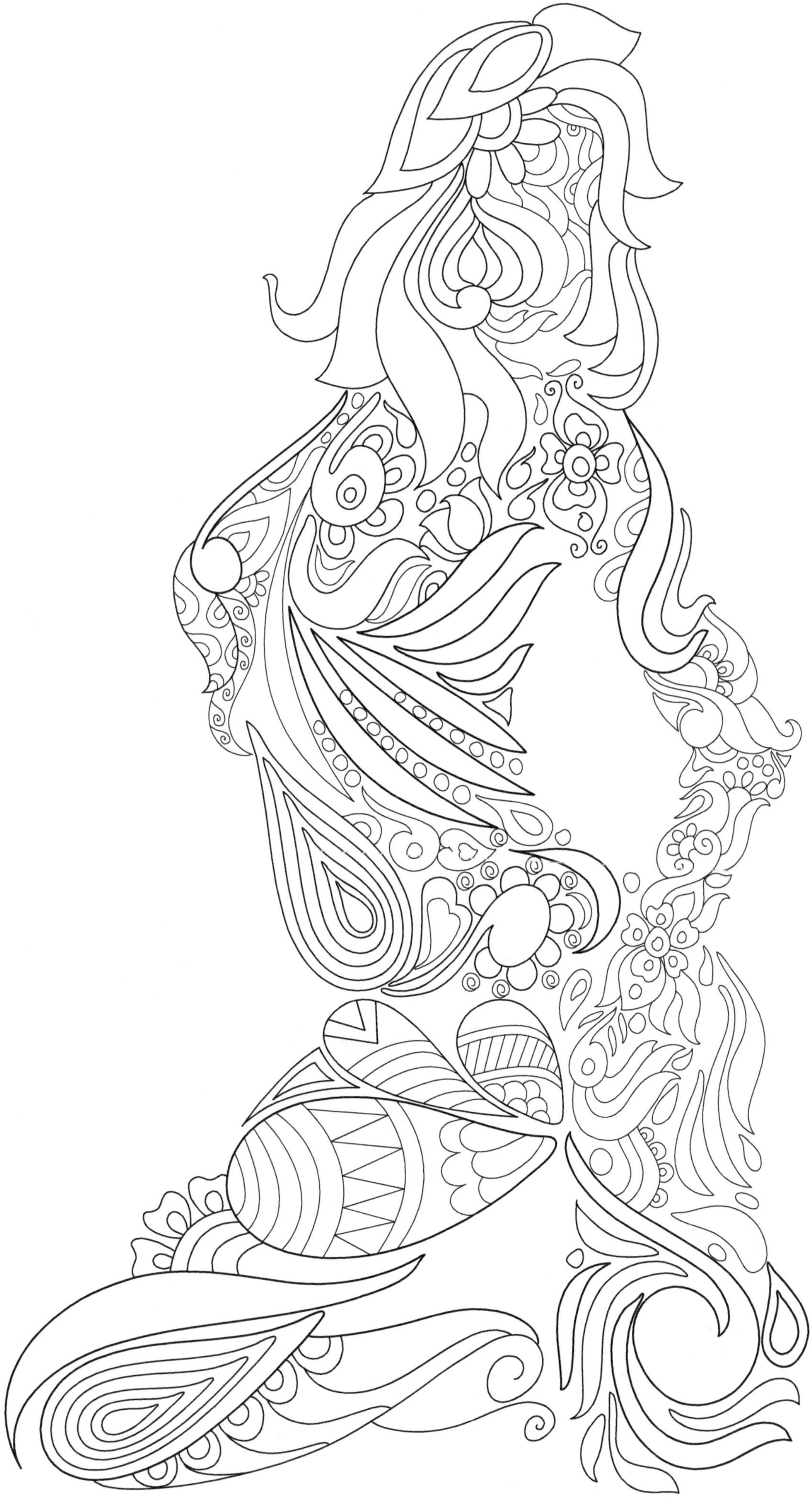

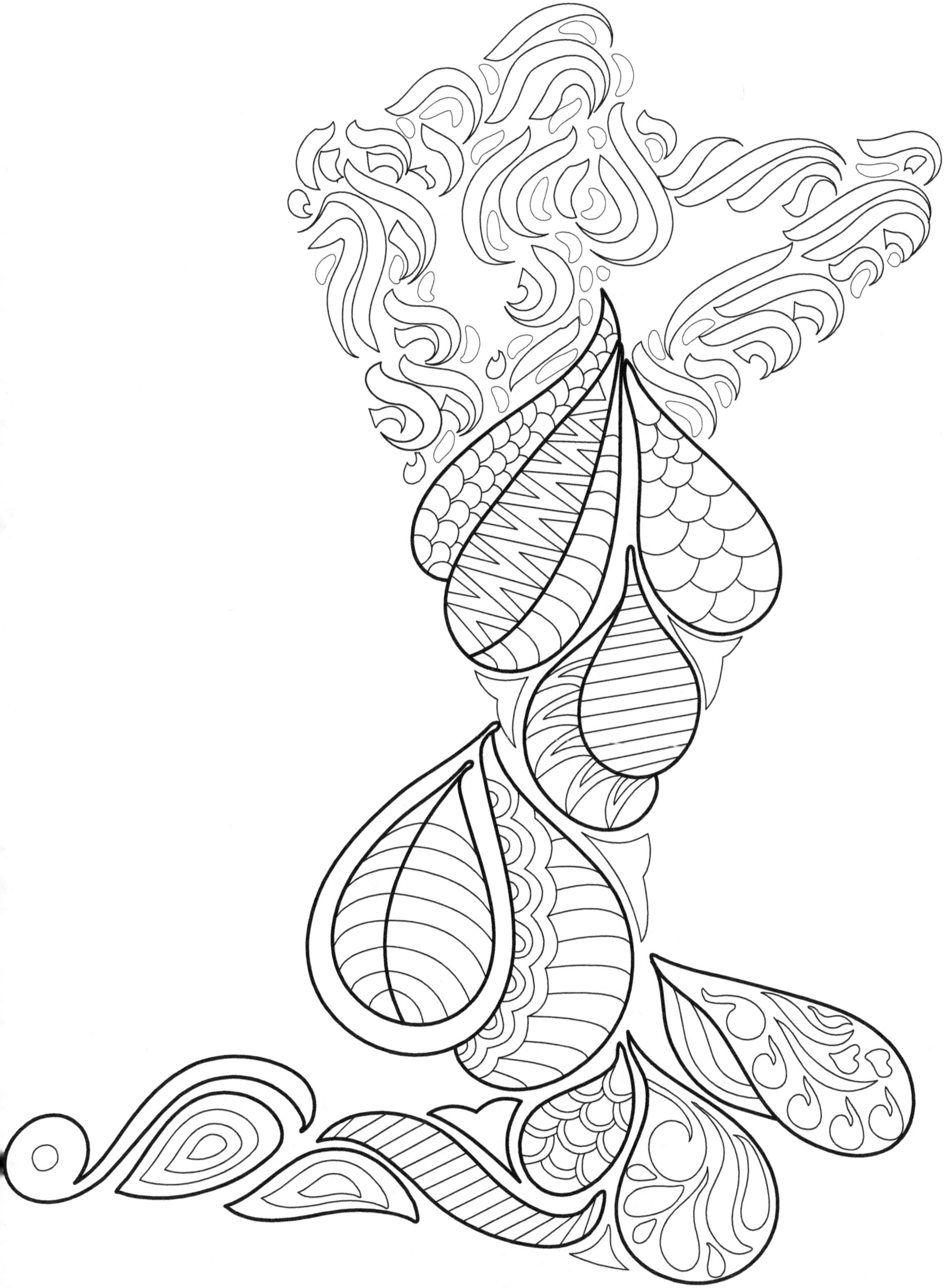

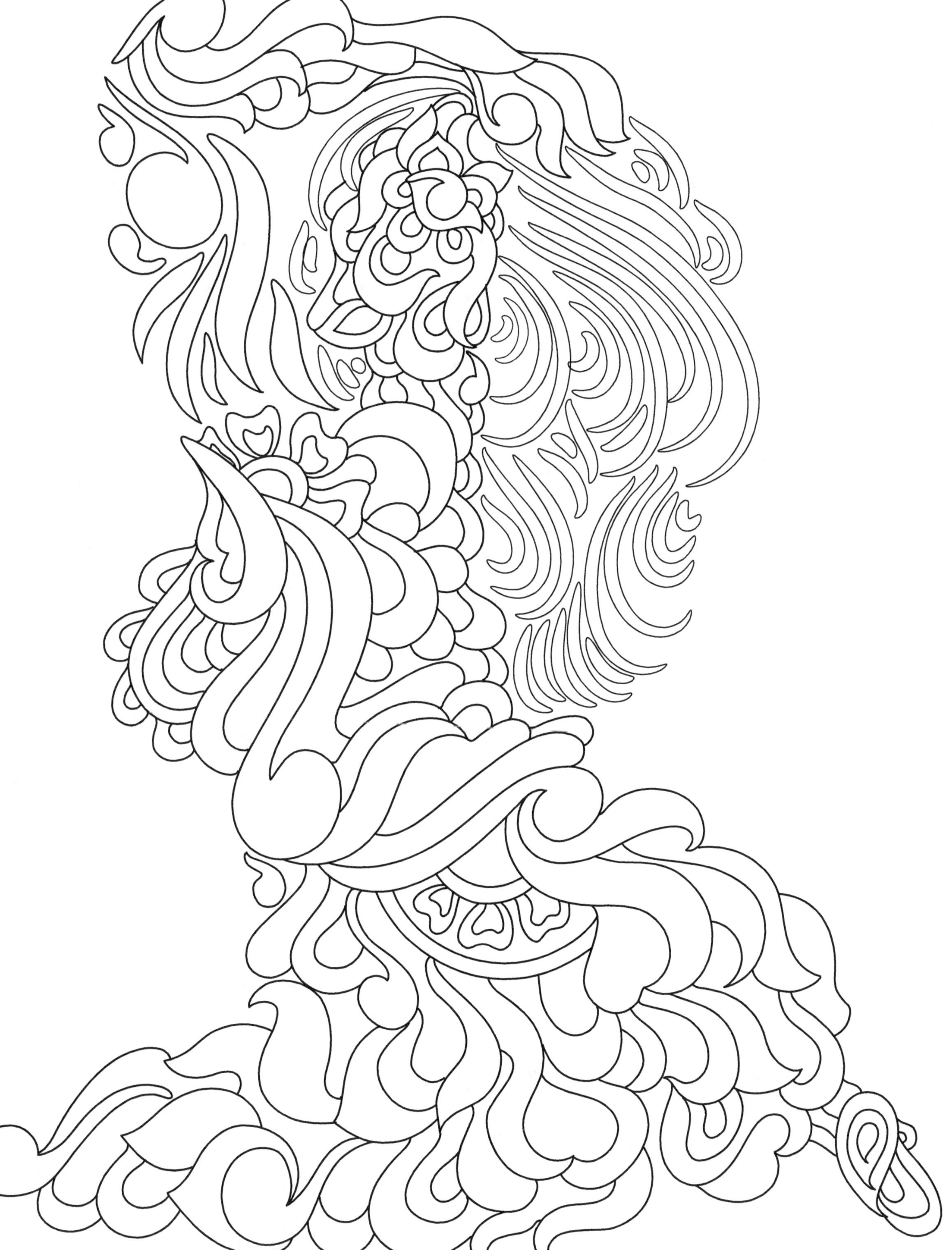

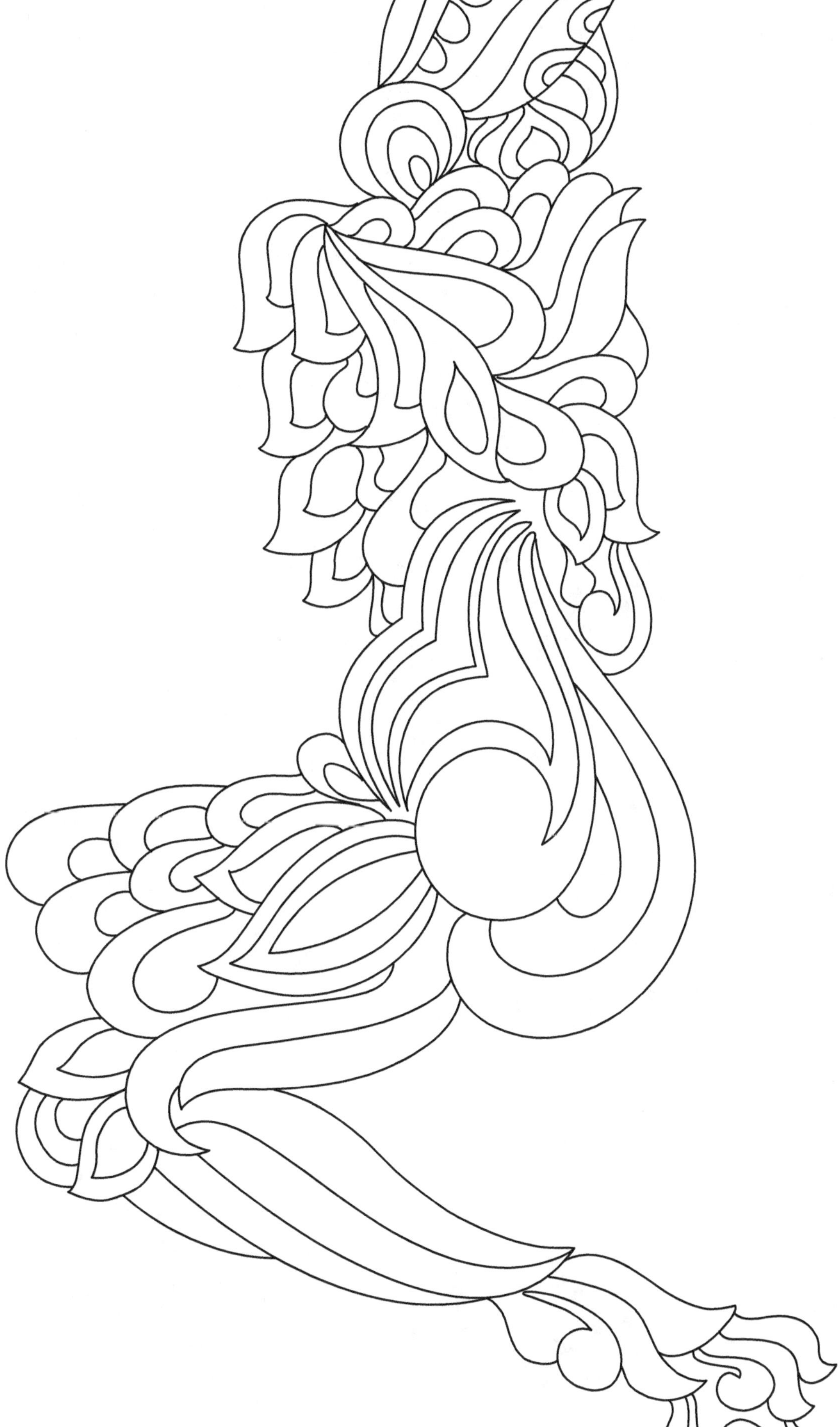

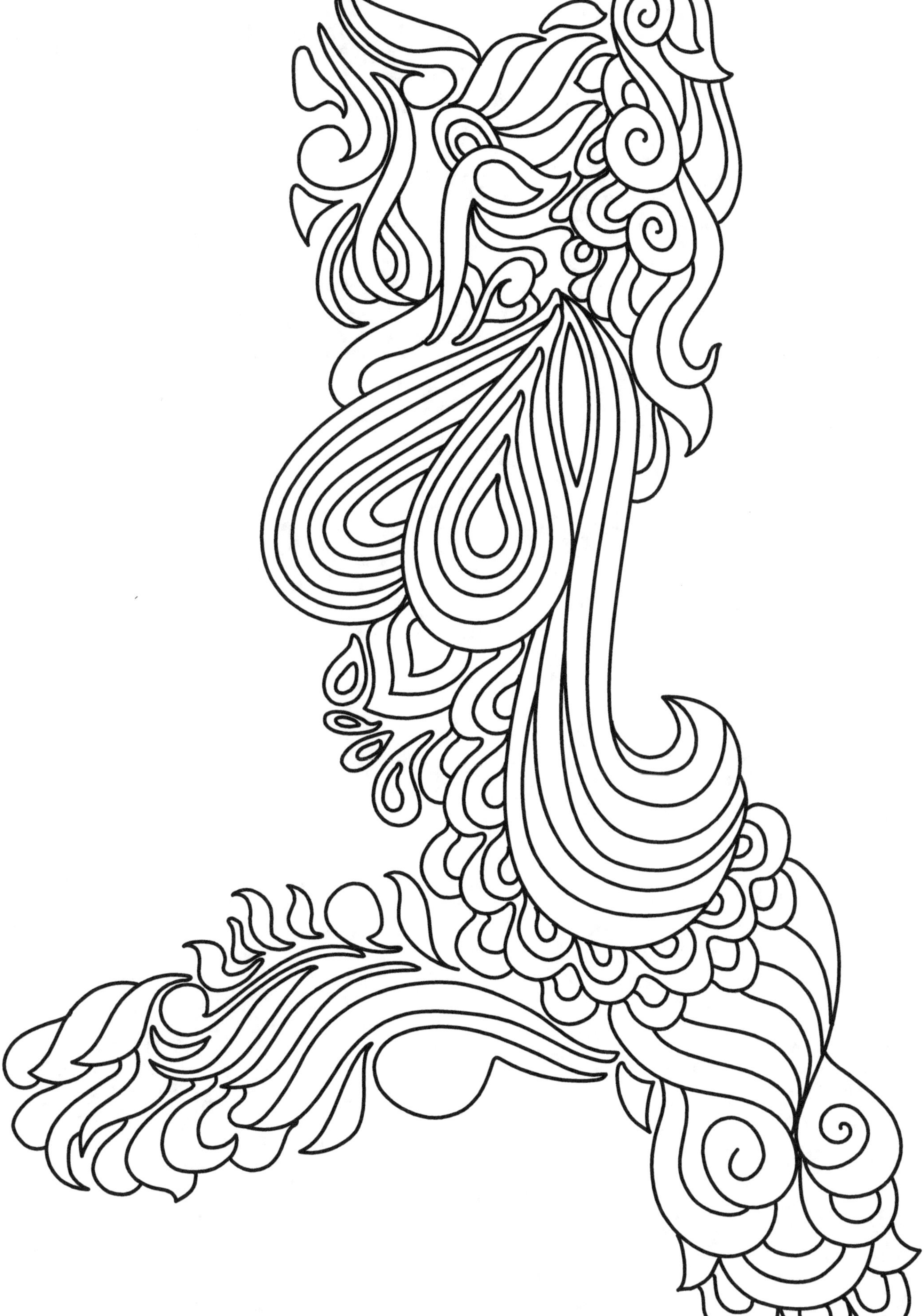

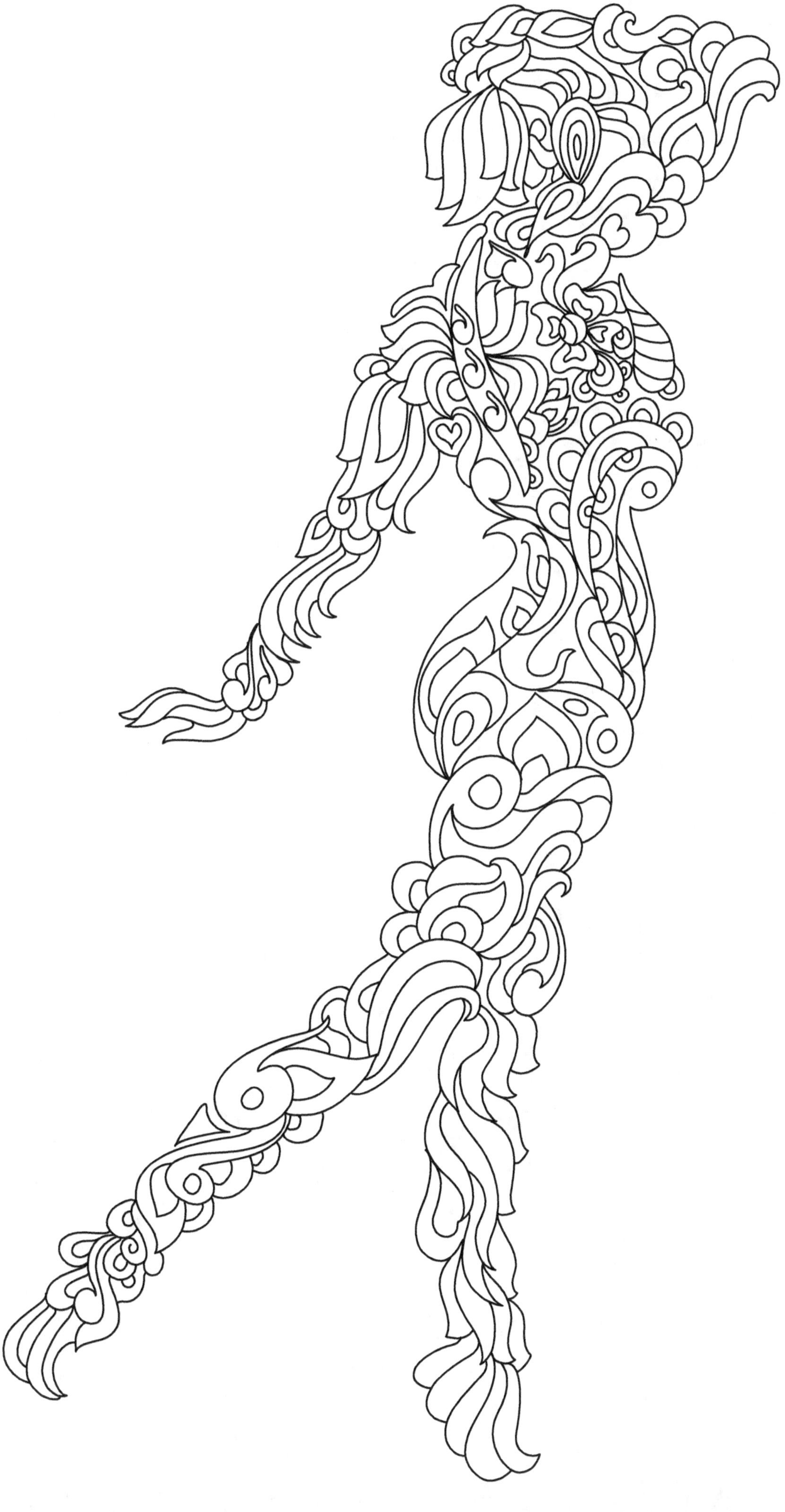

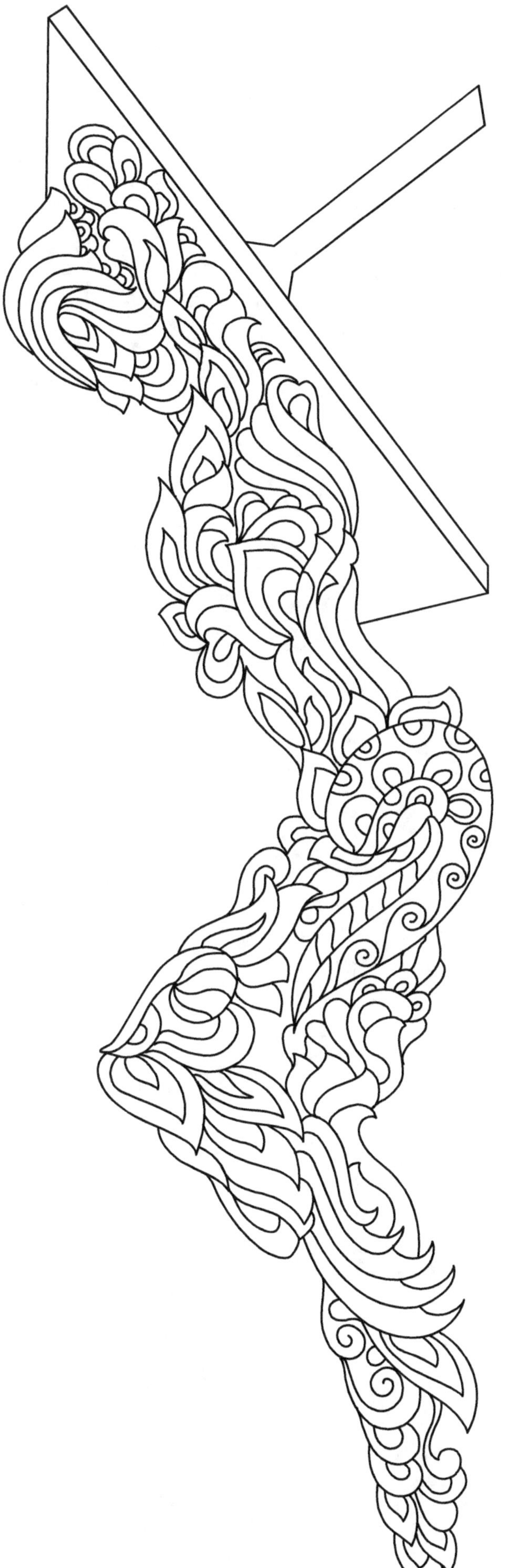

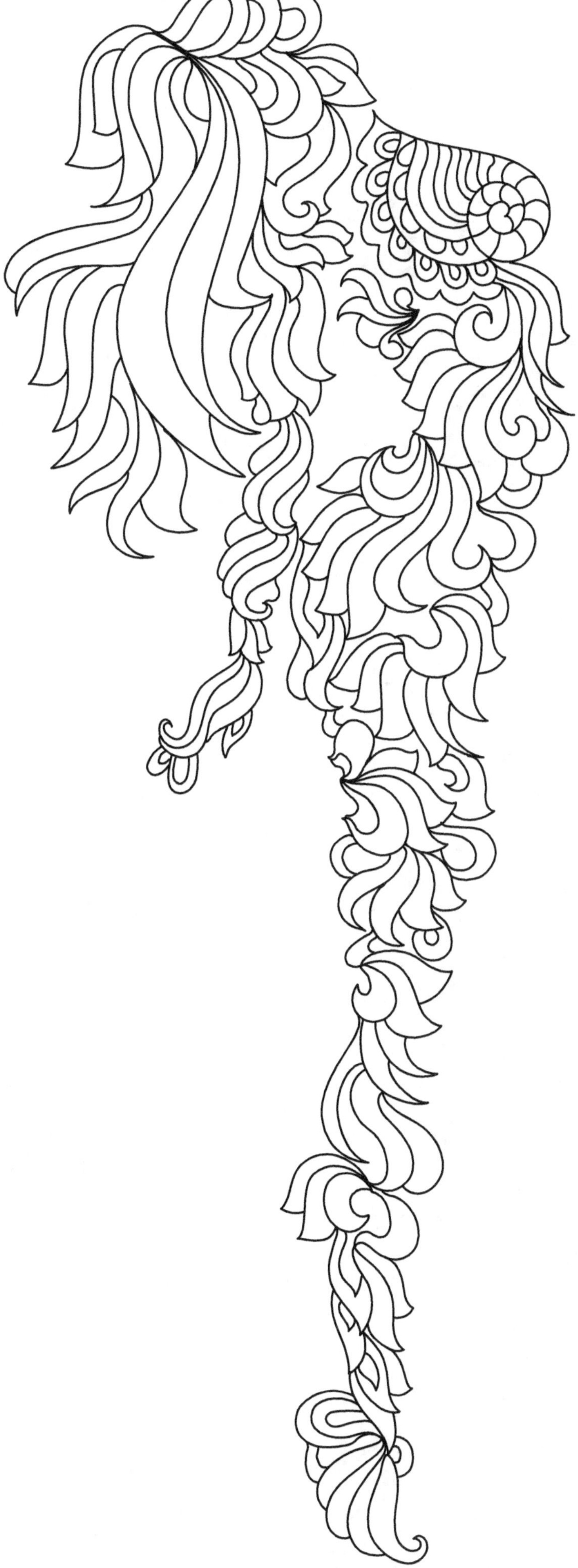

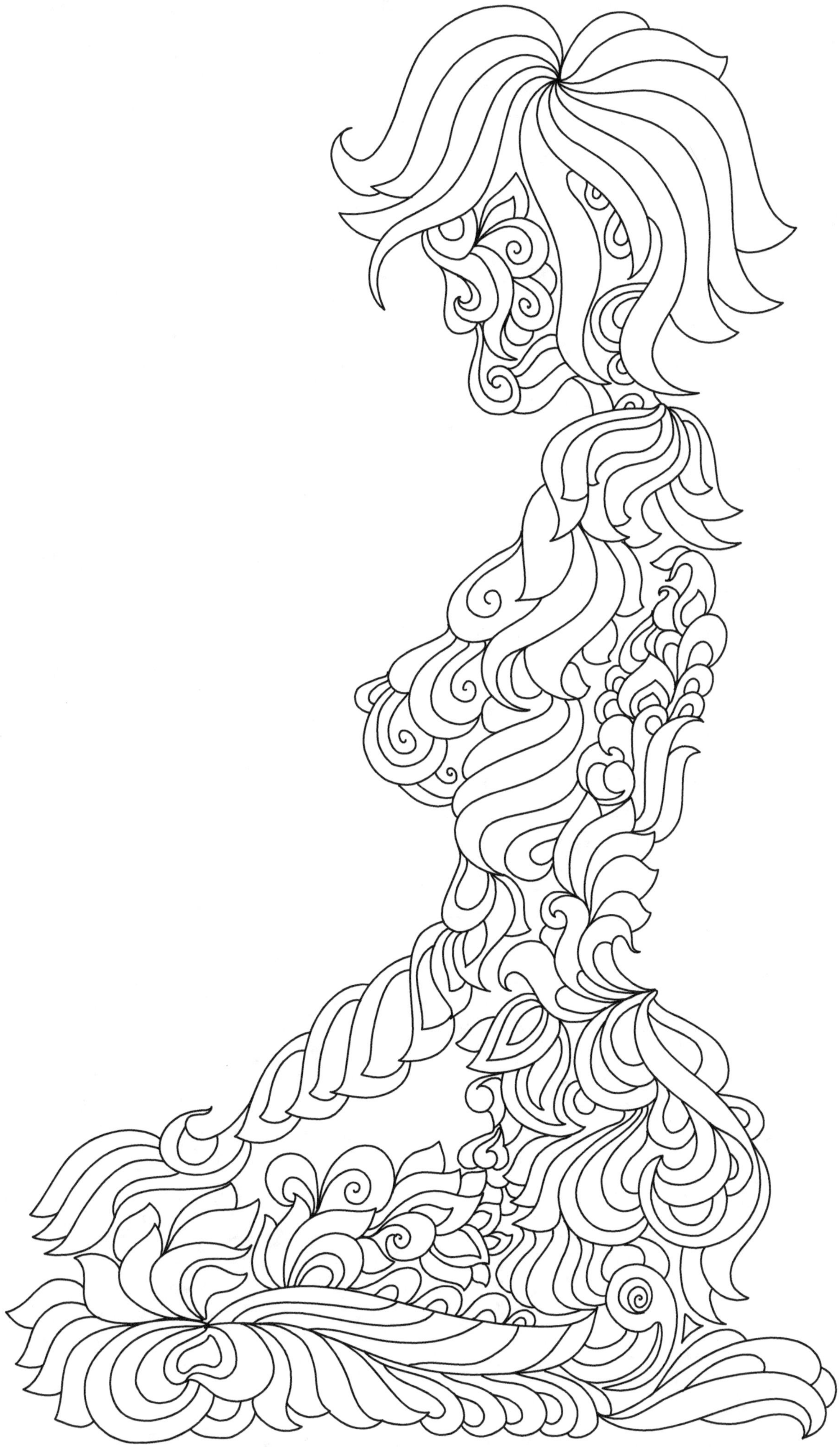

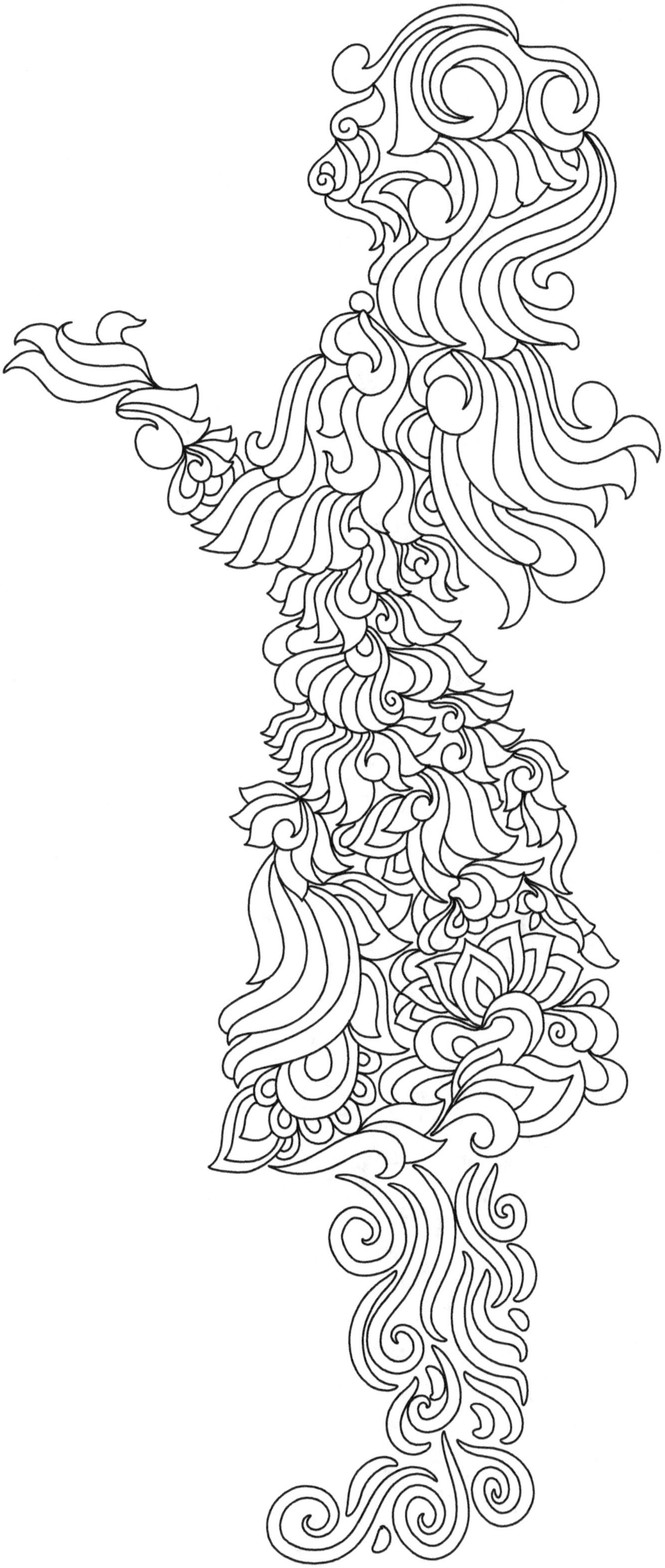

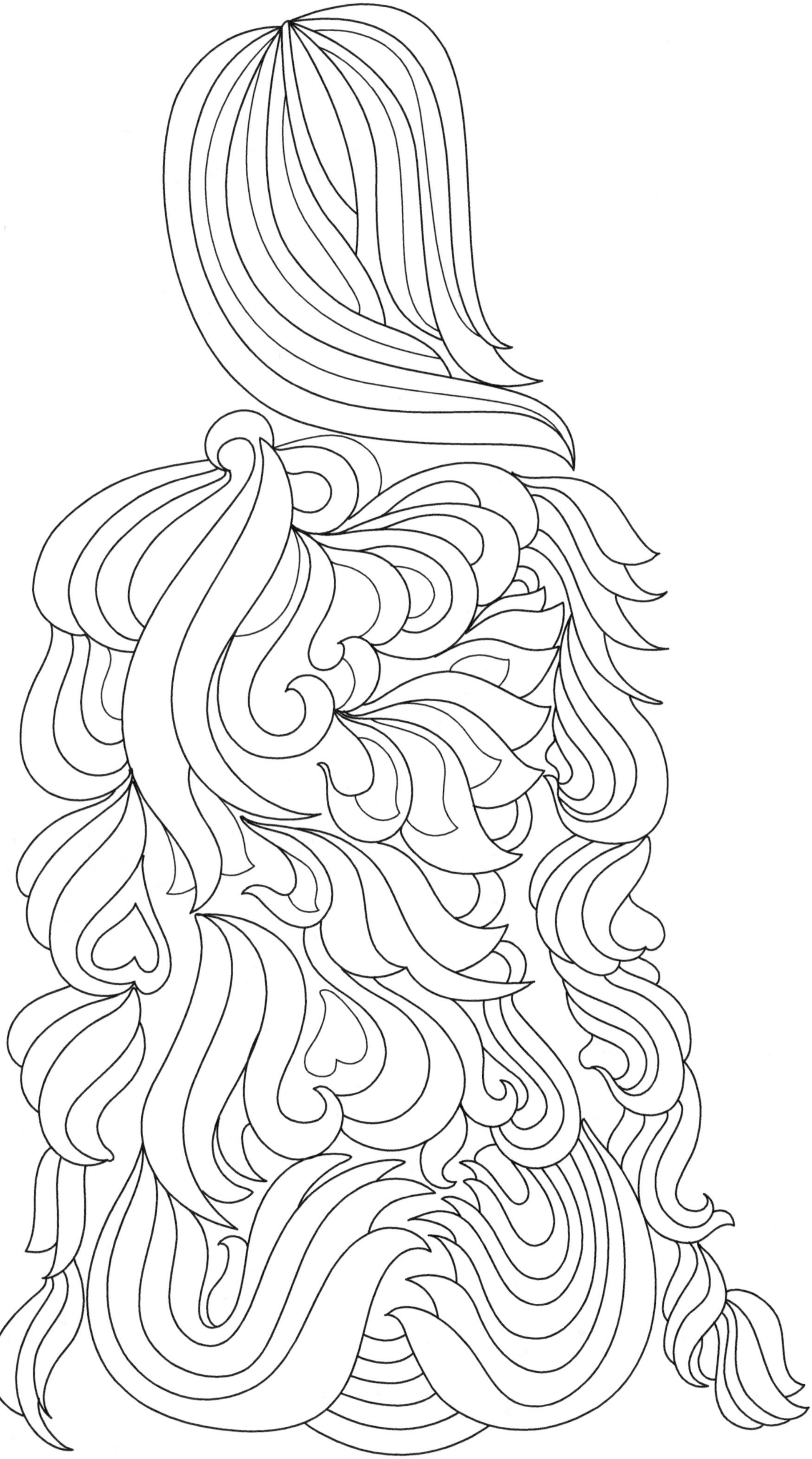

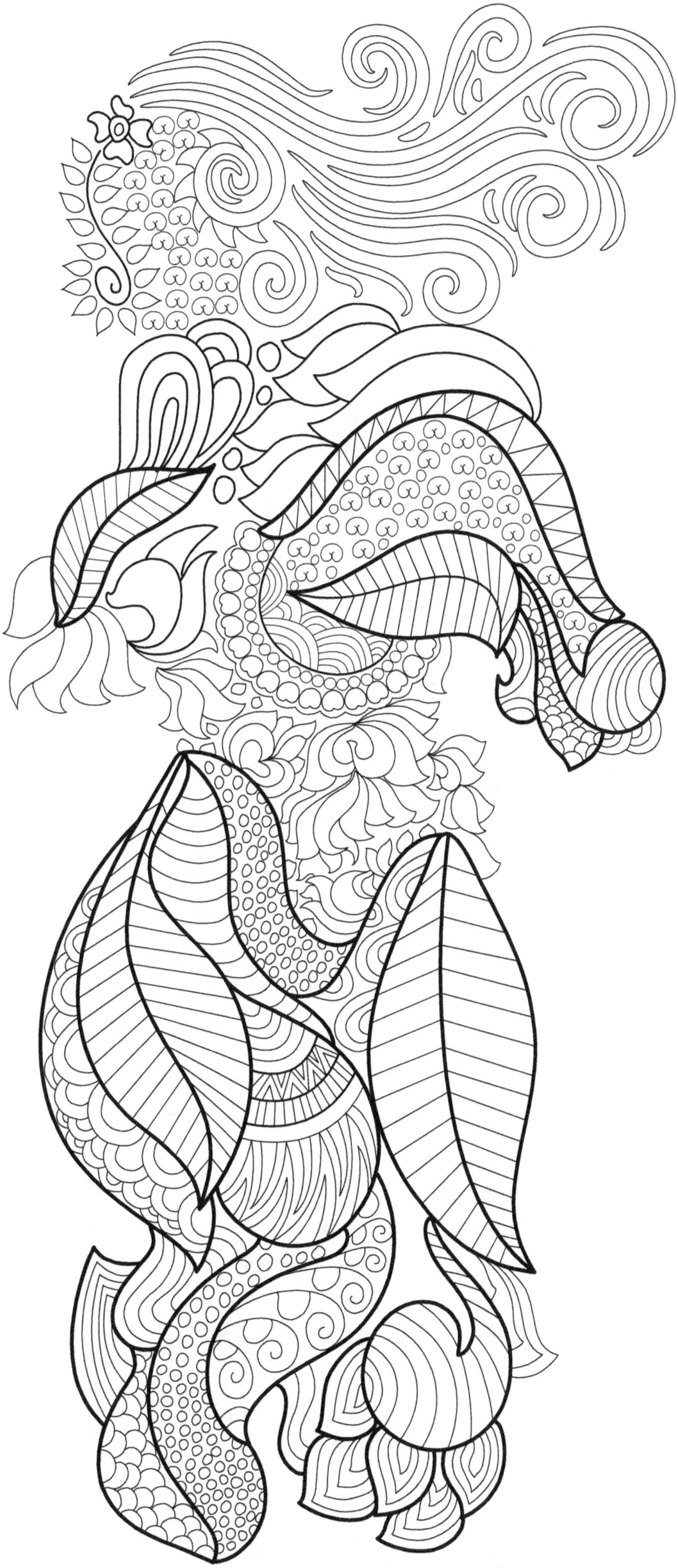

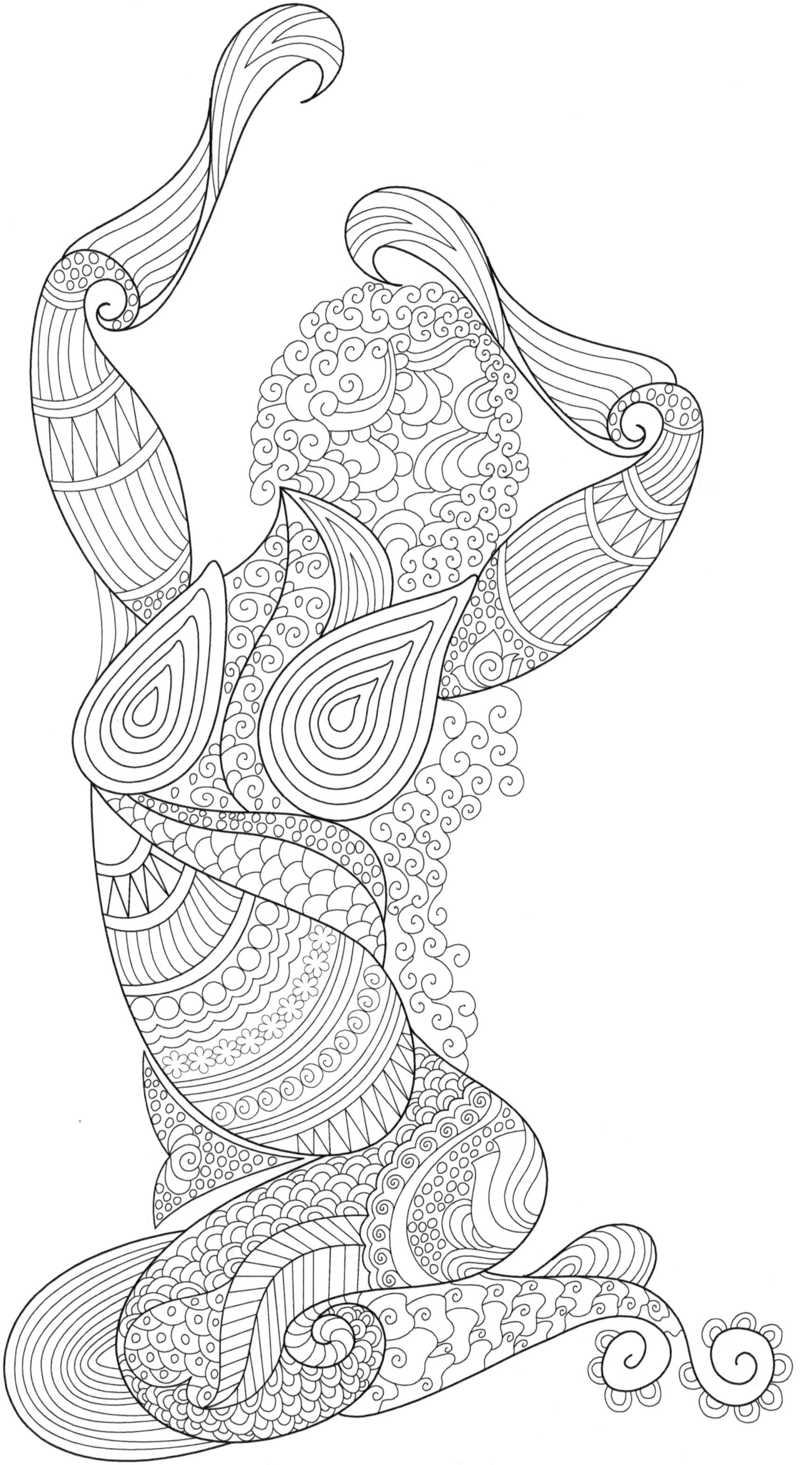

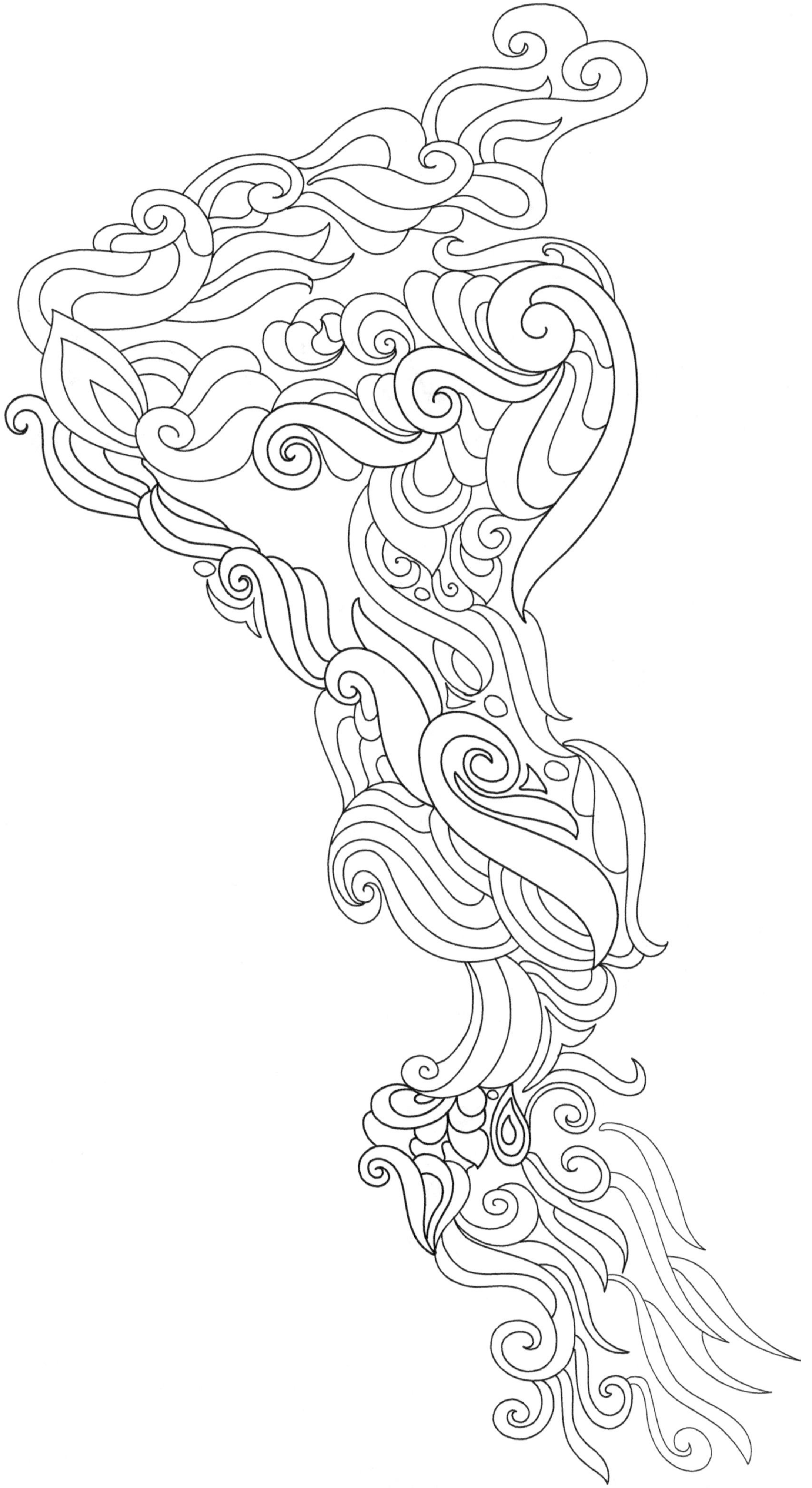

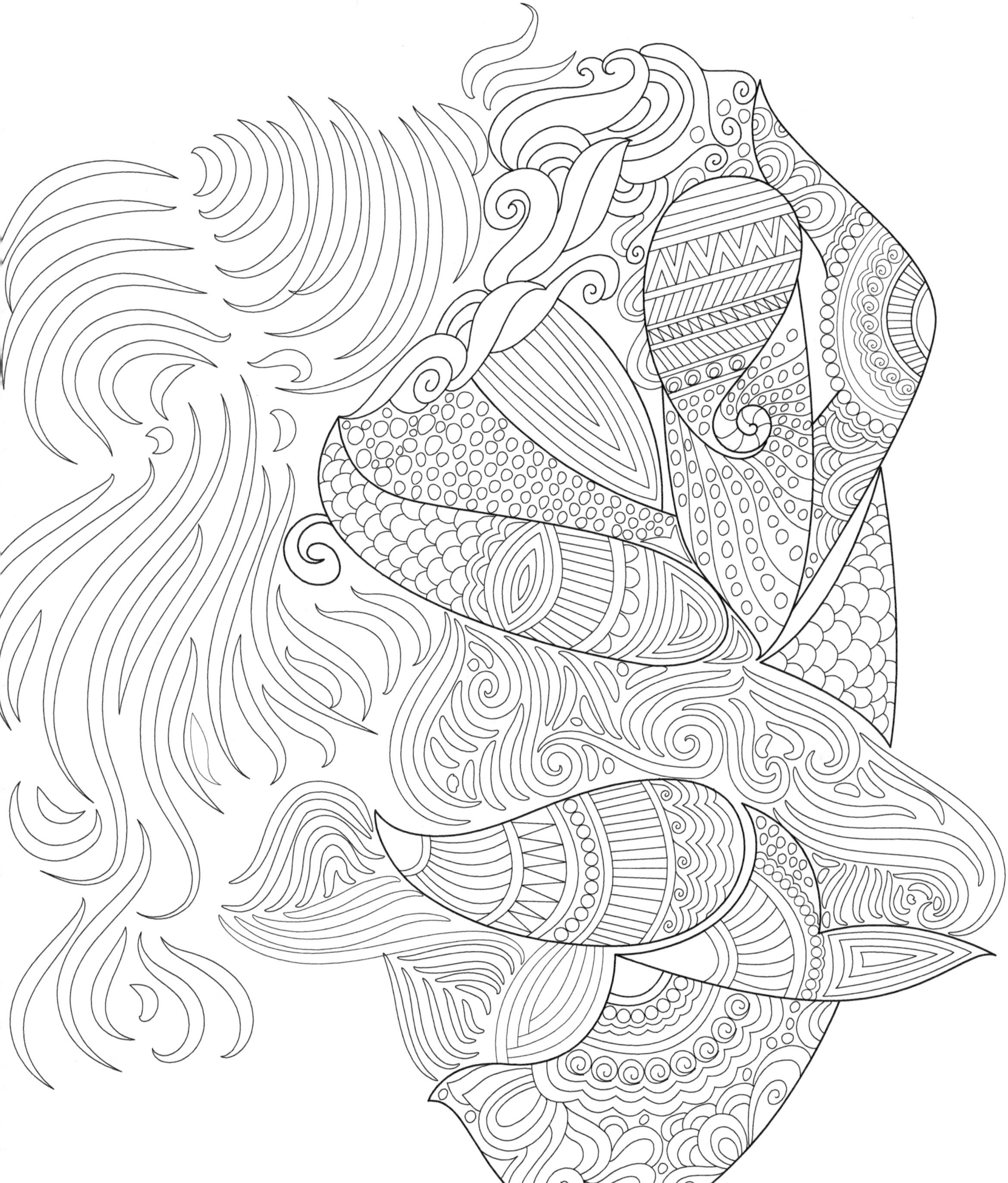

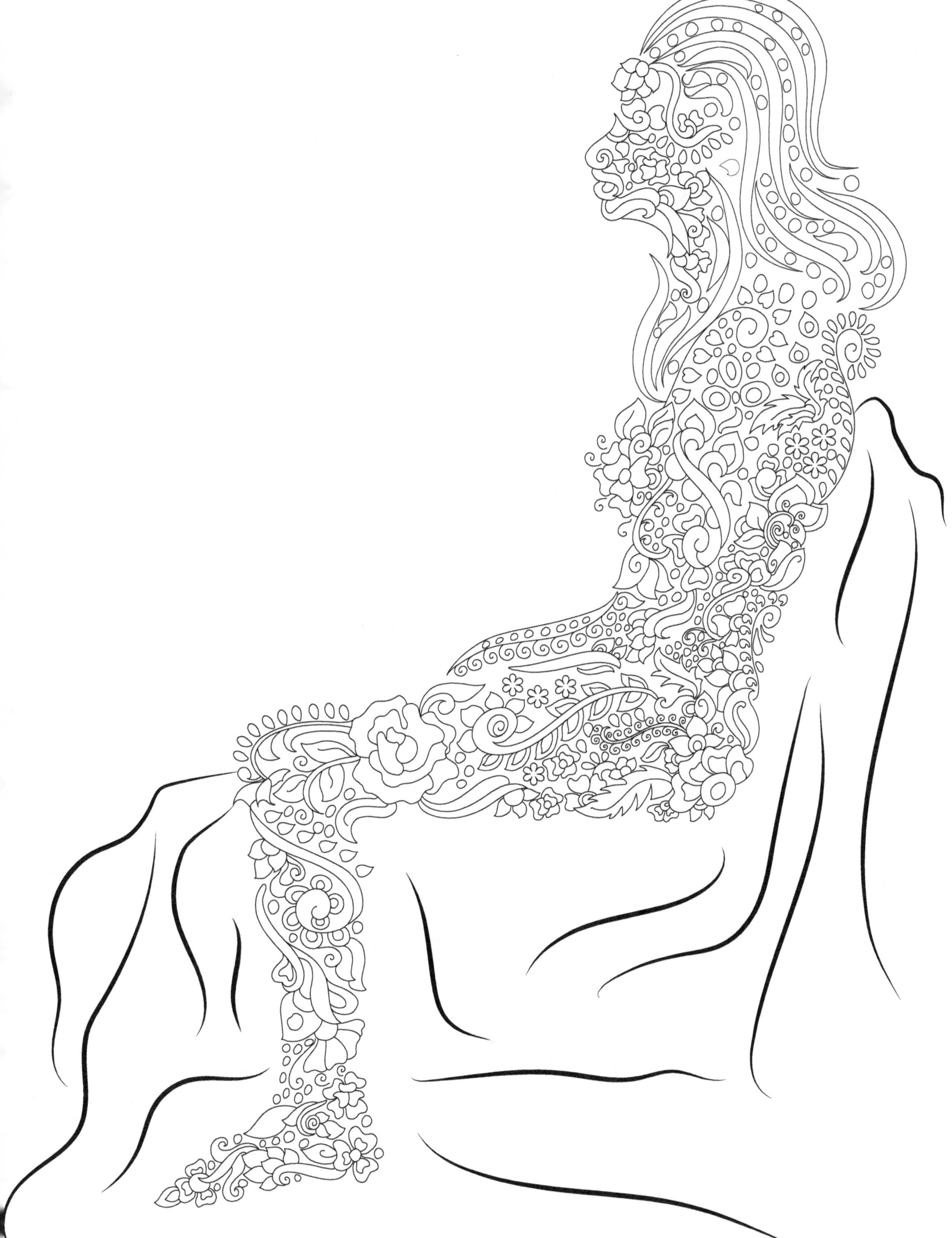

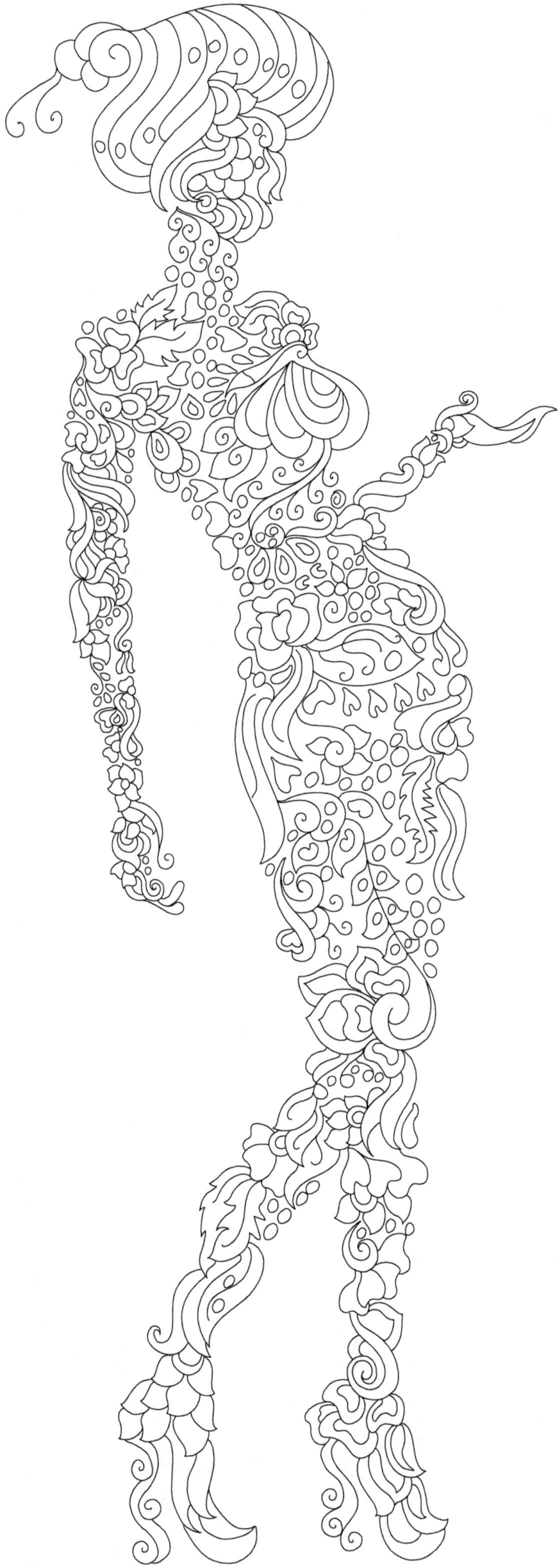

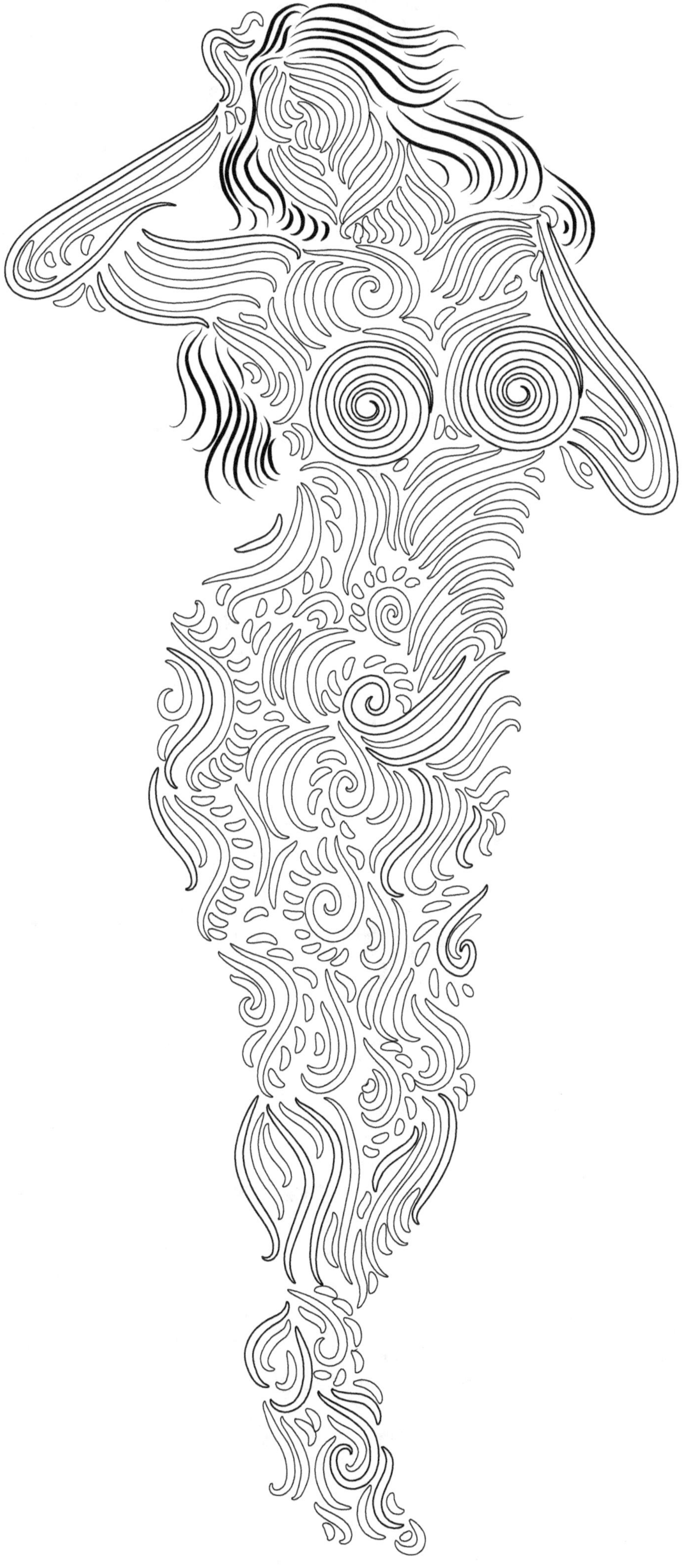

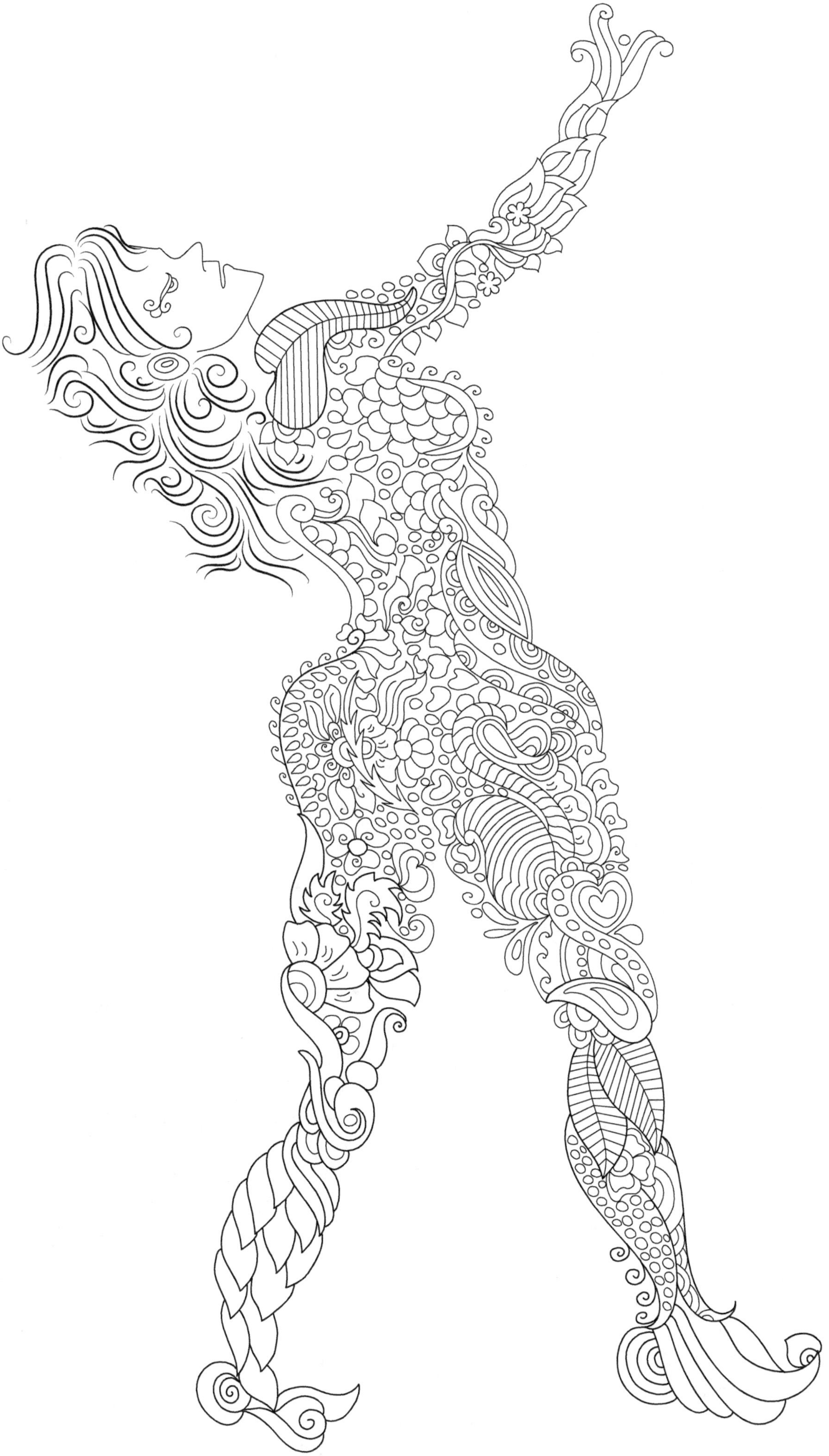

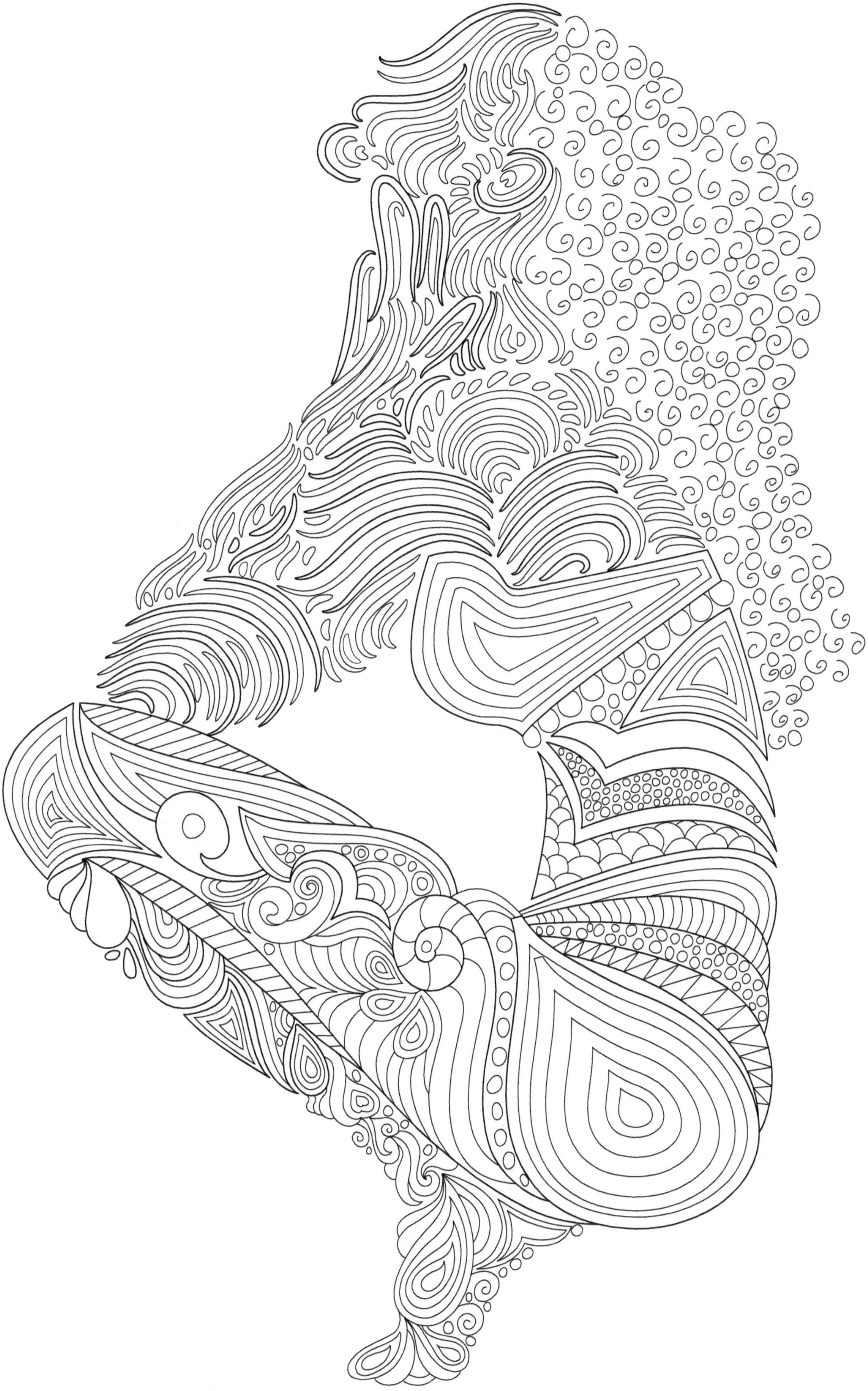

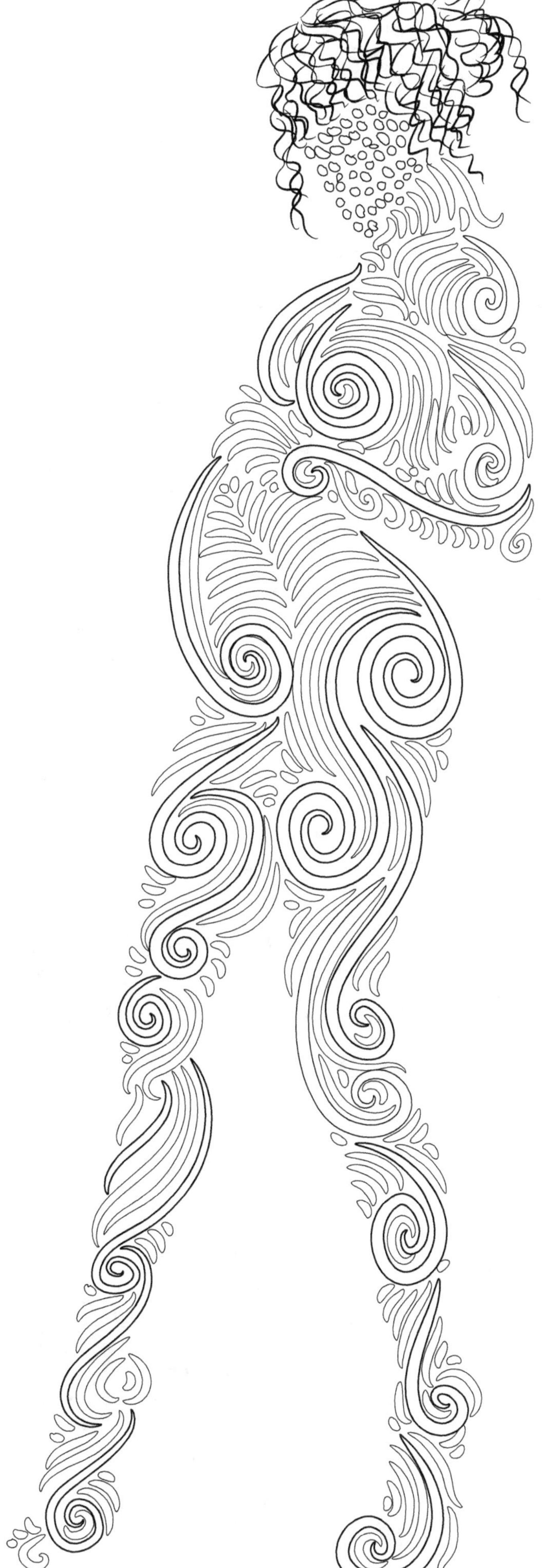

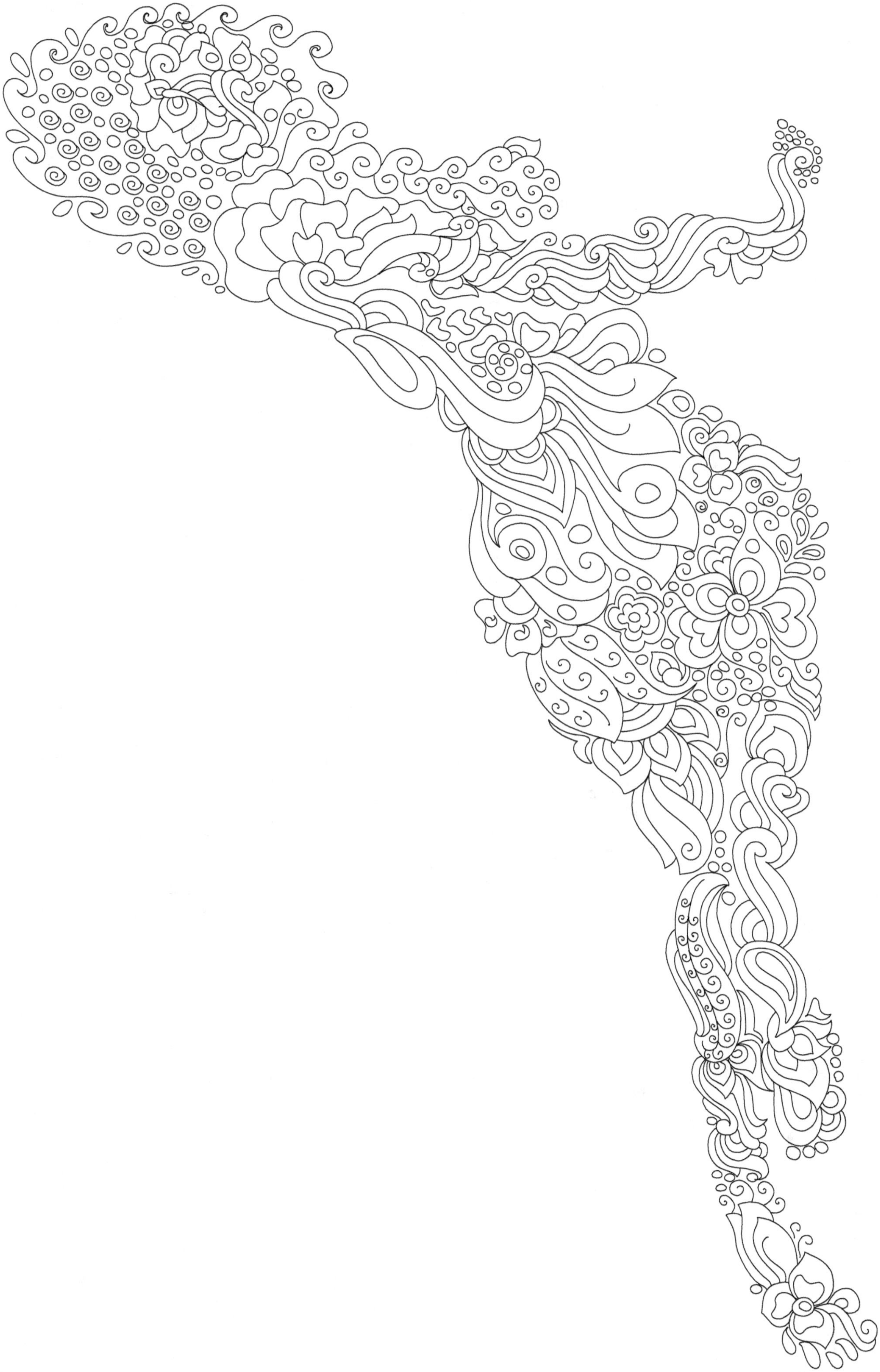

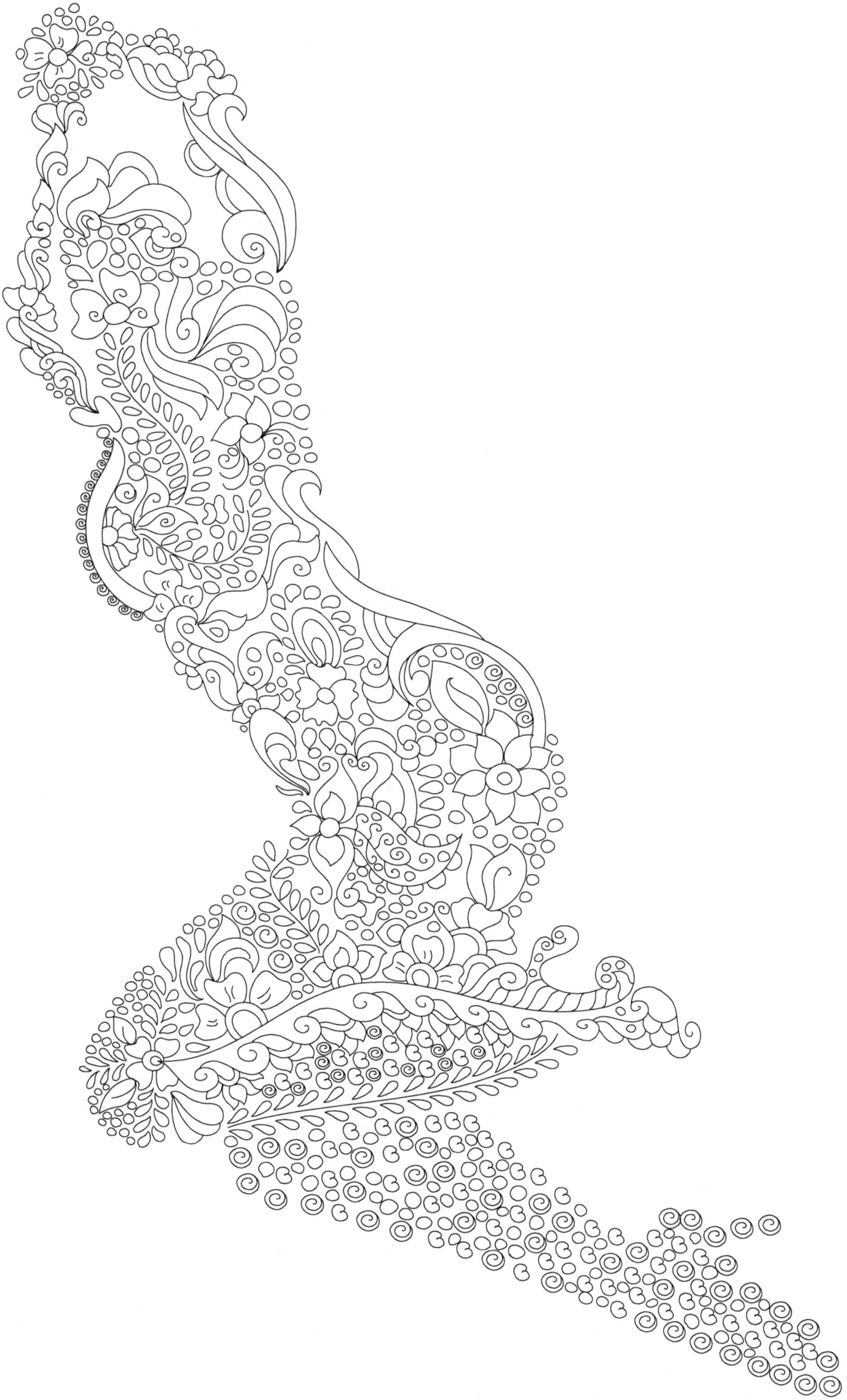

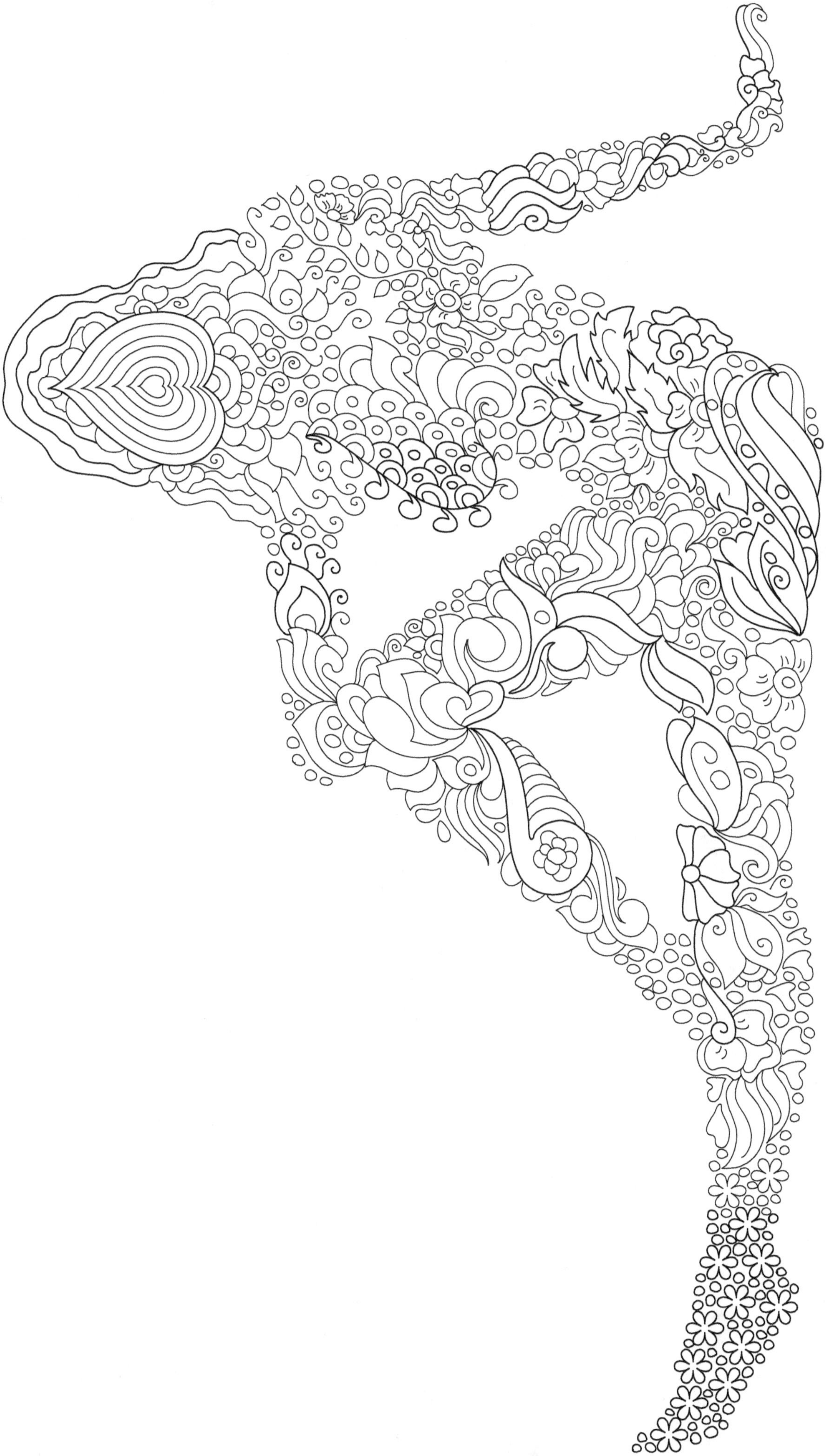

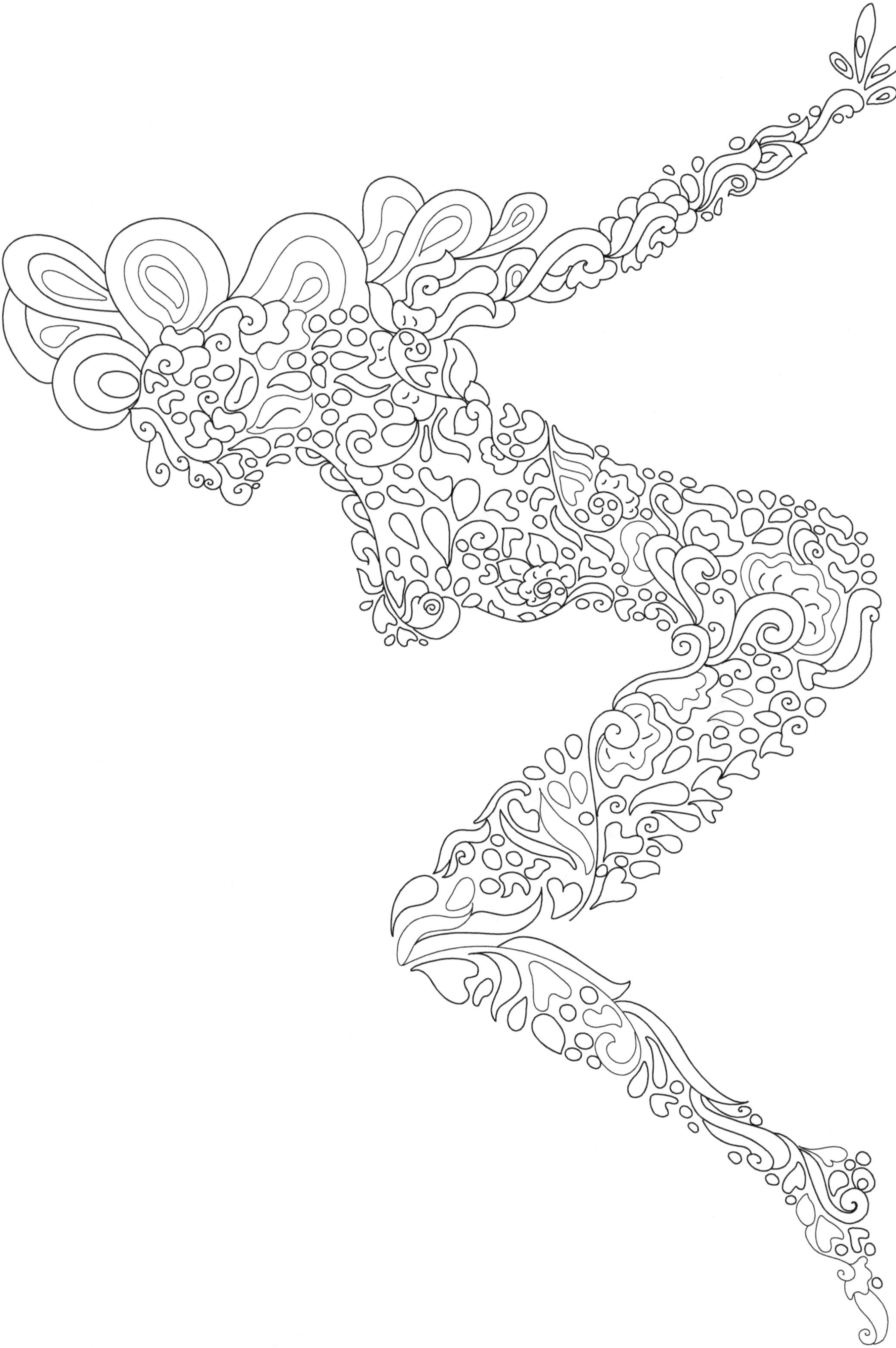

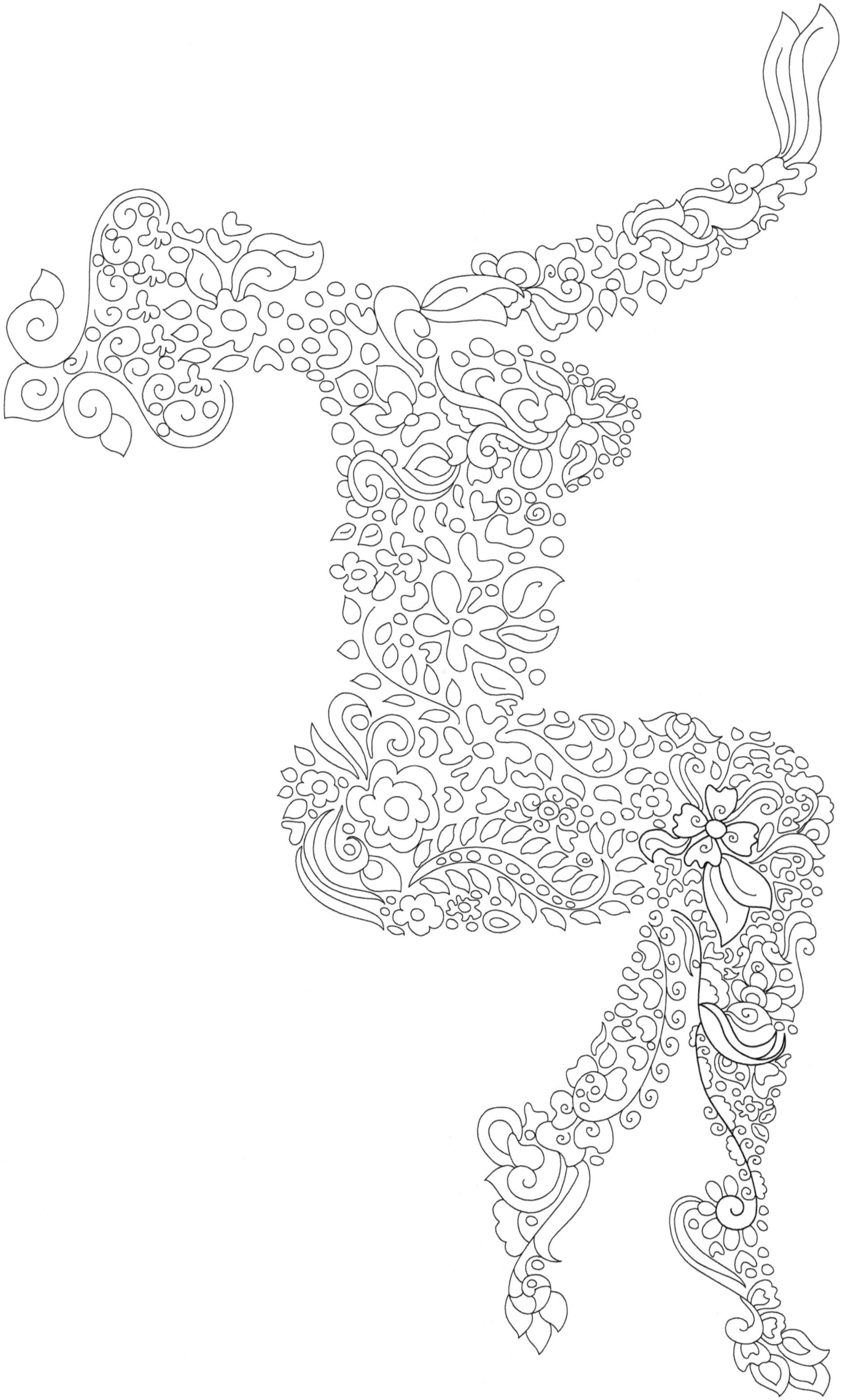

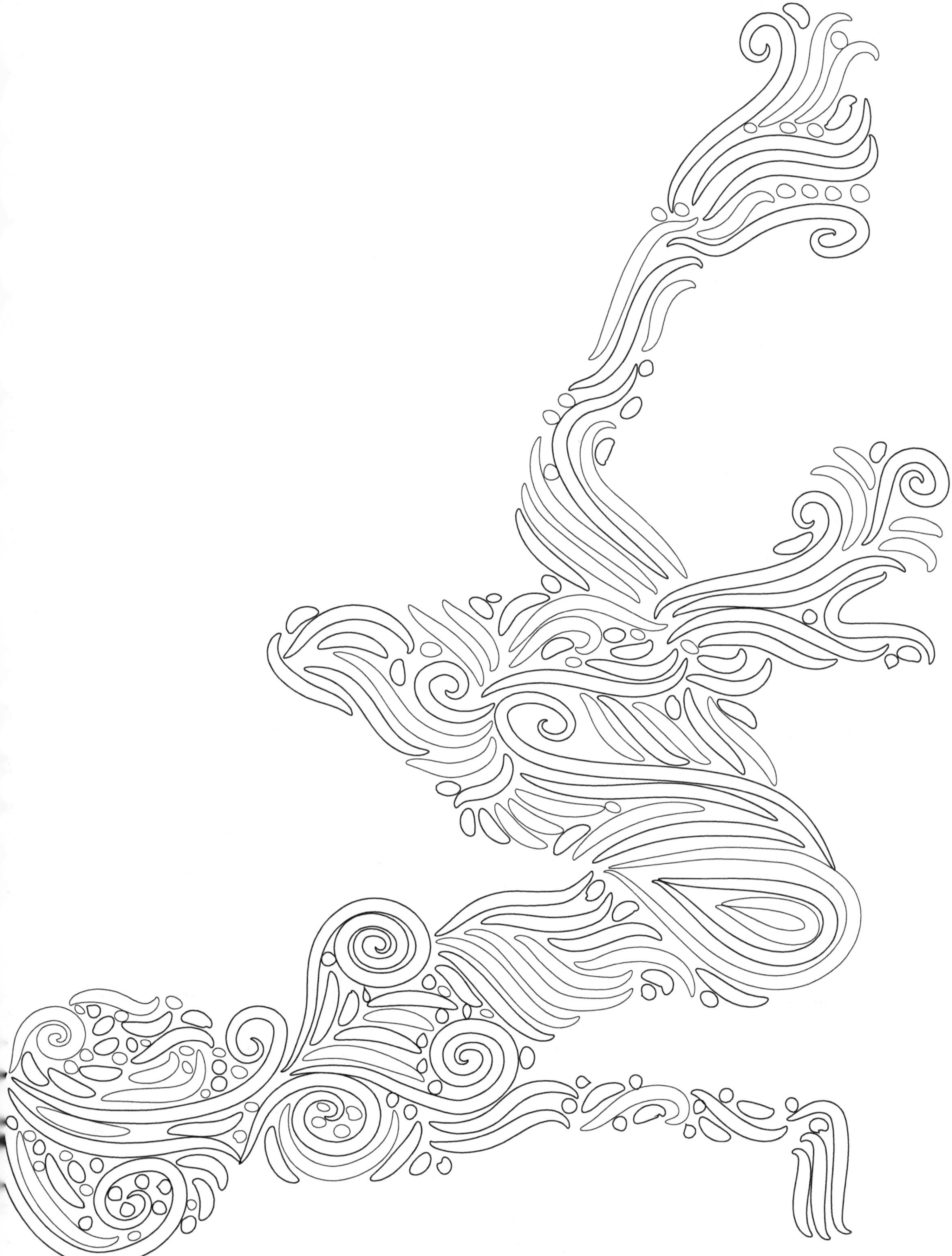

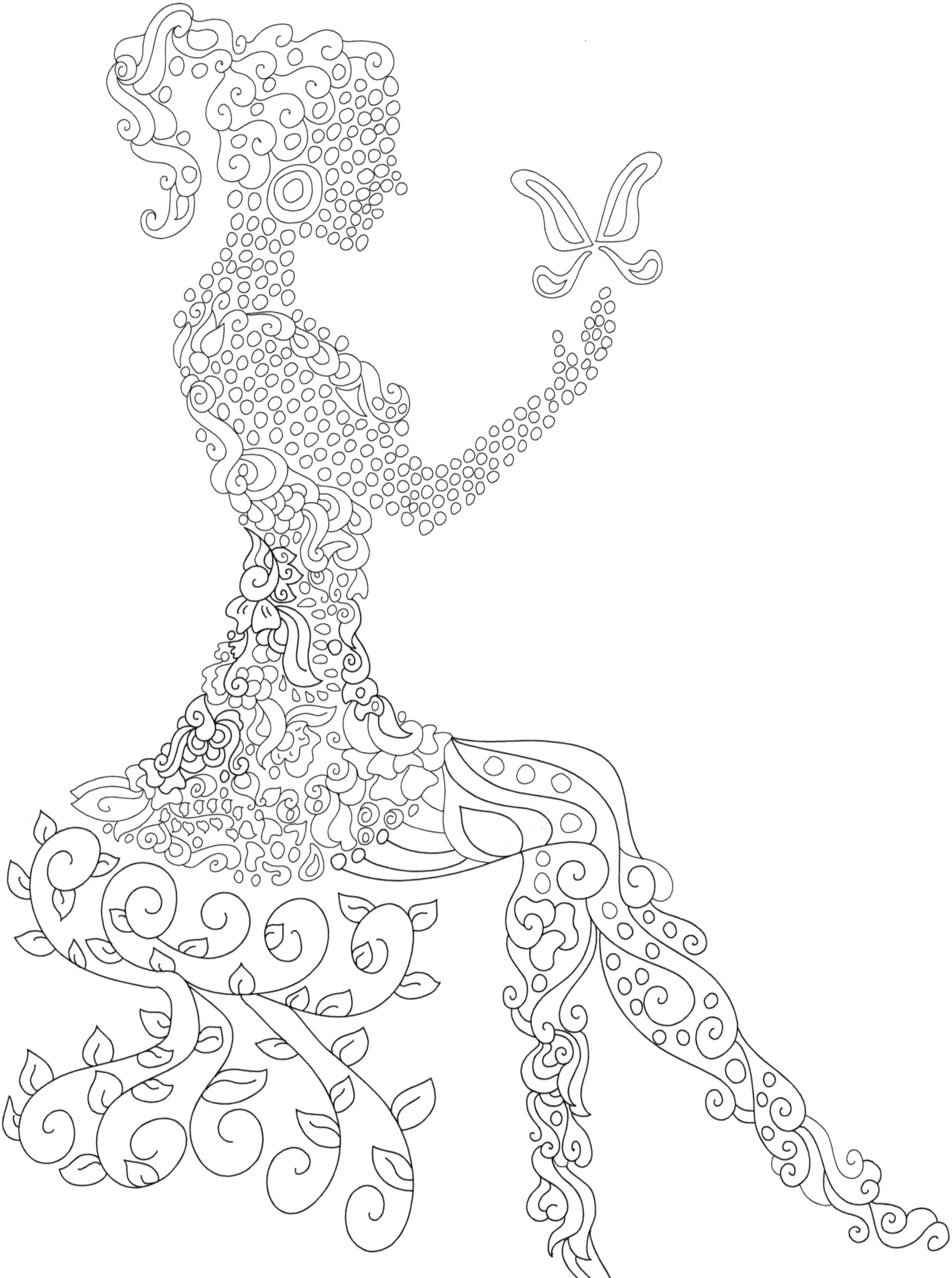

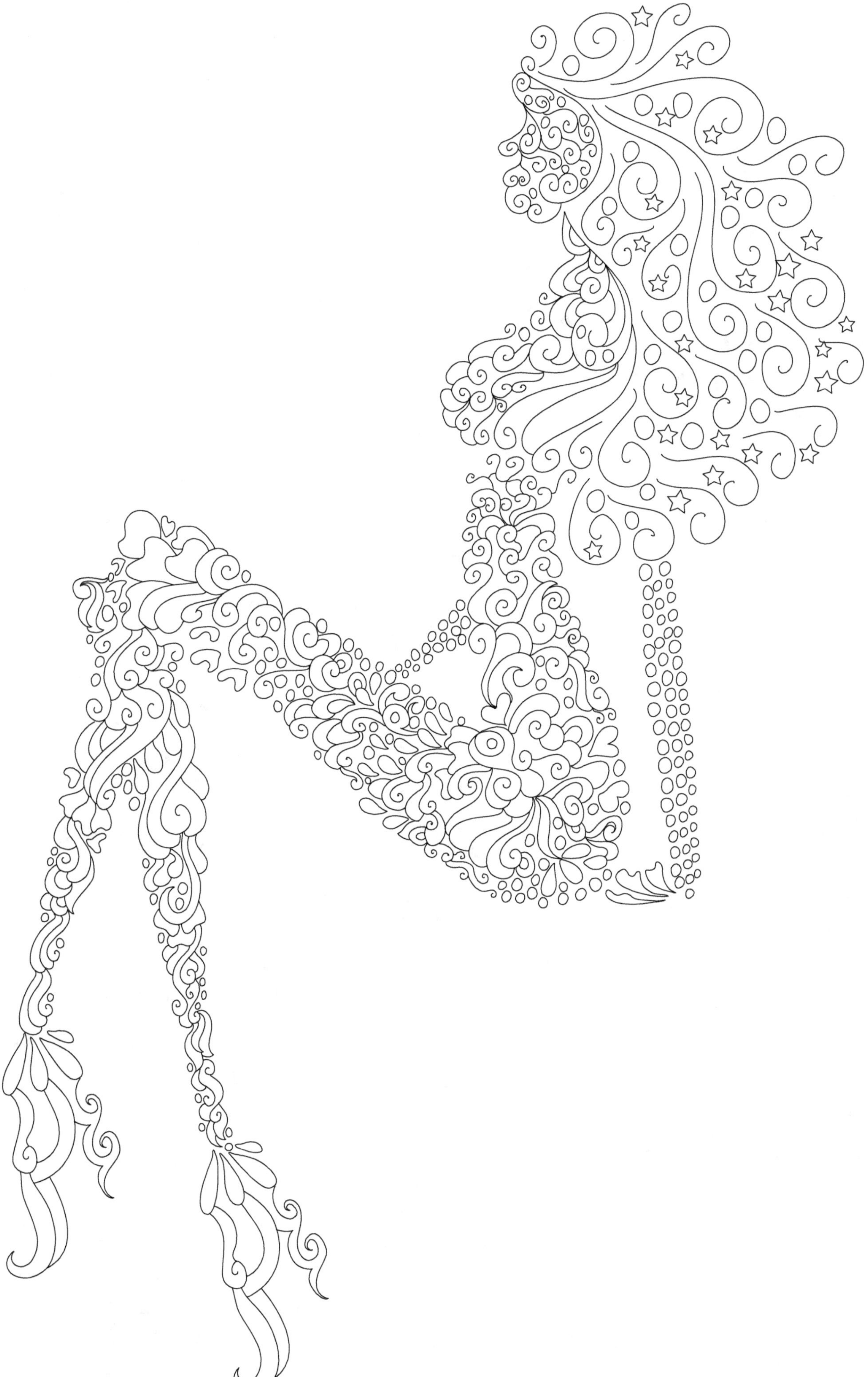

MAZE

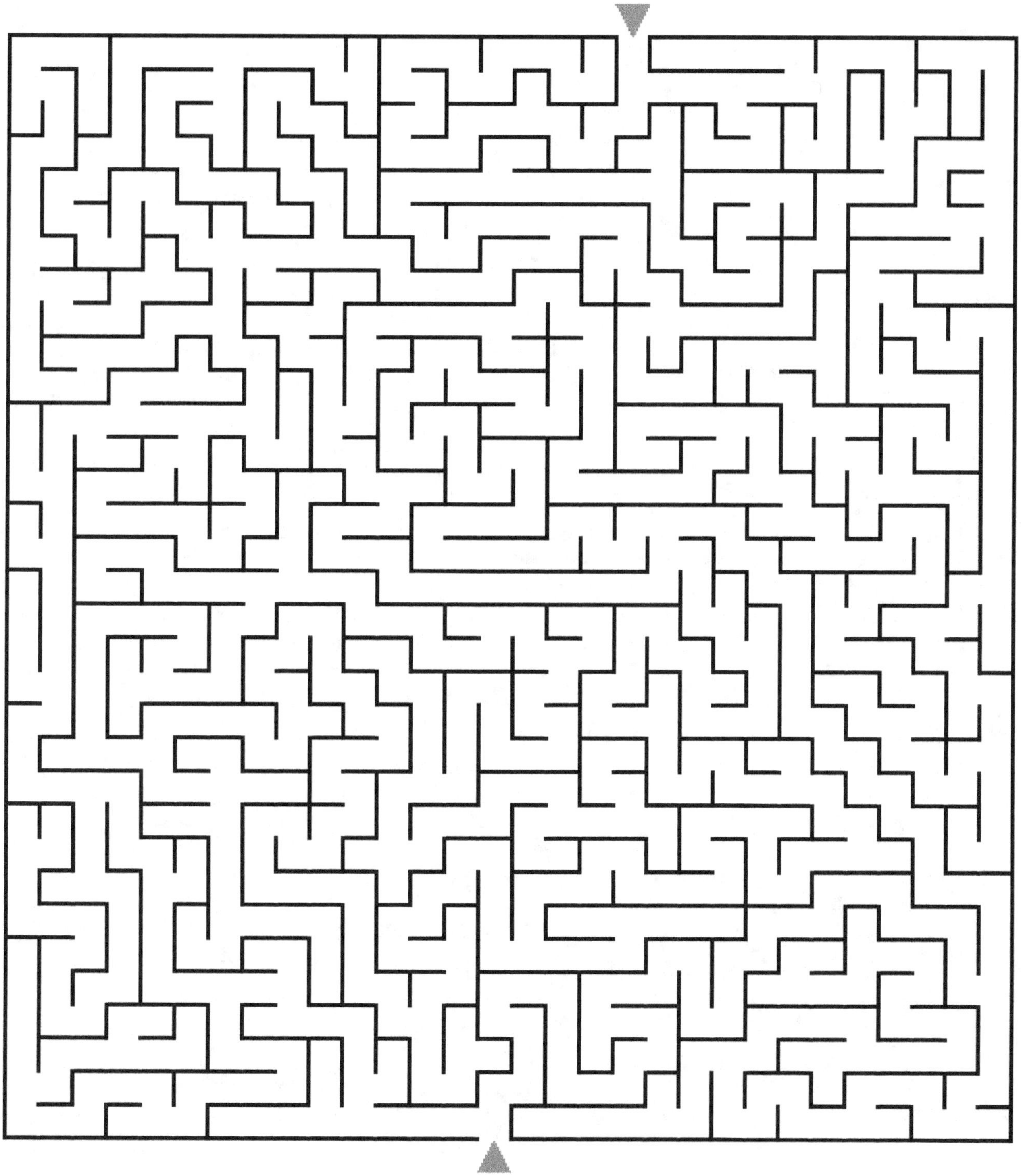

COLOR CHARTS

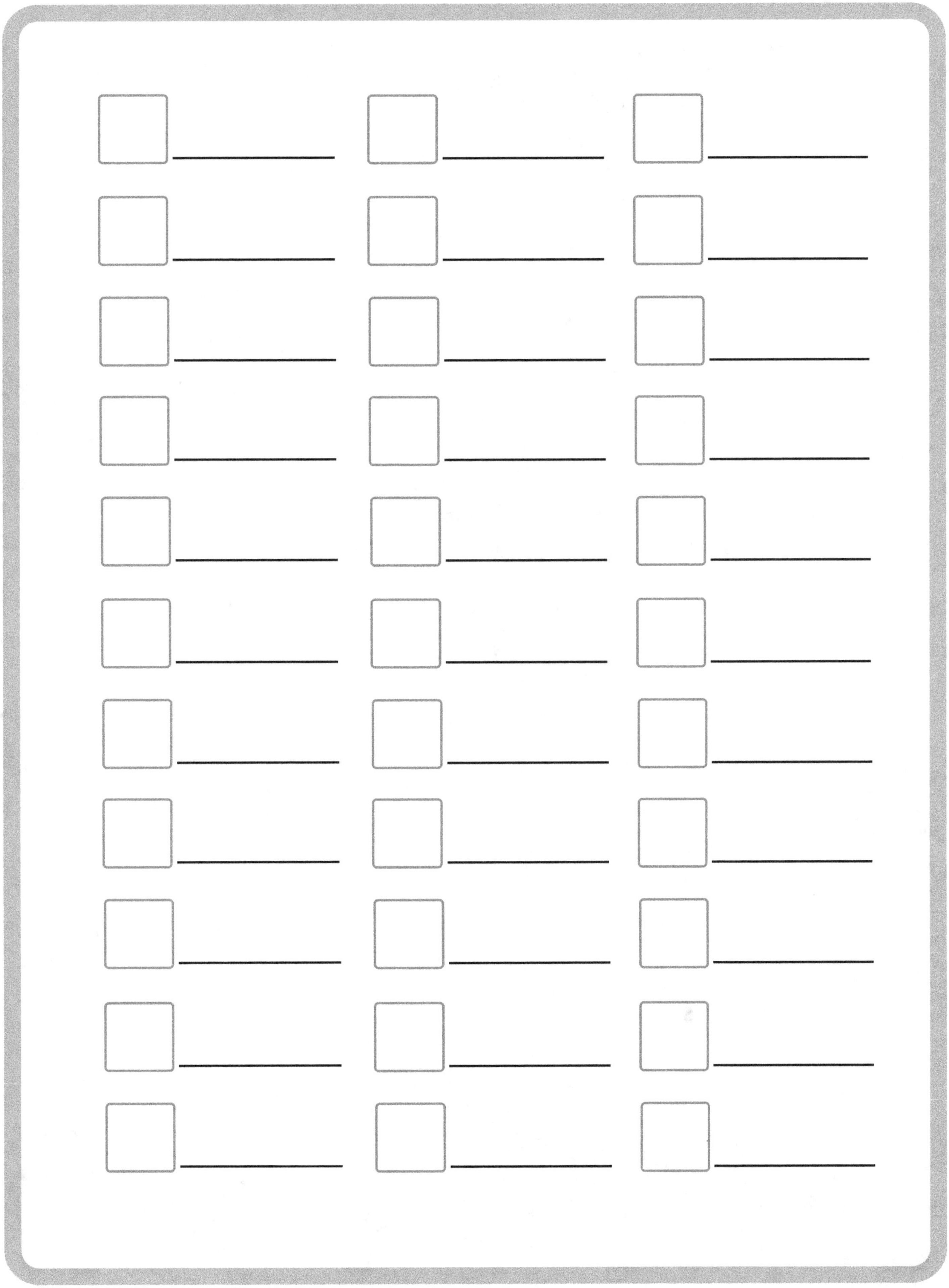

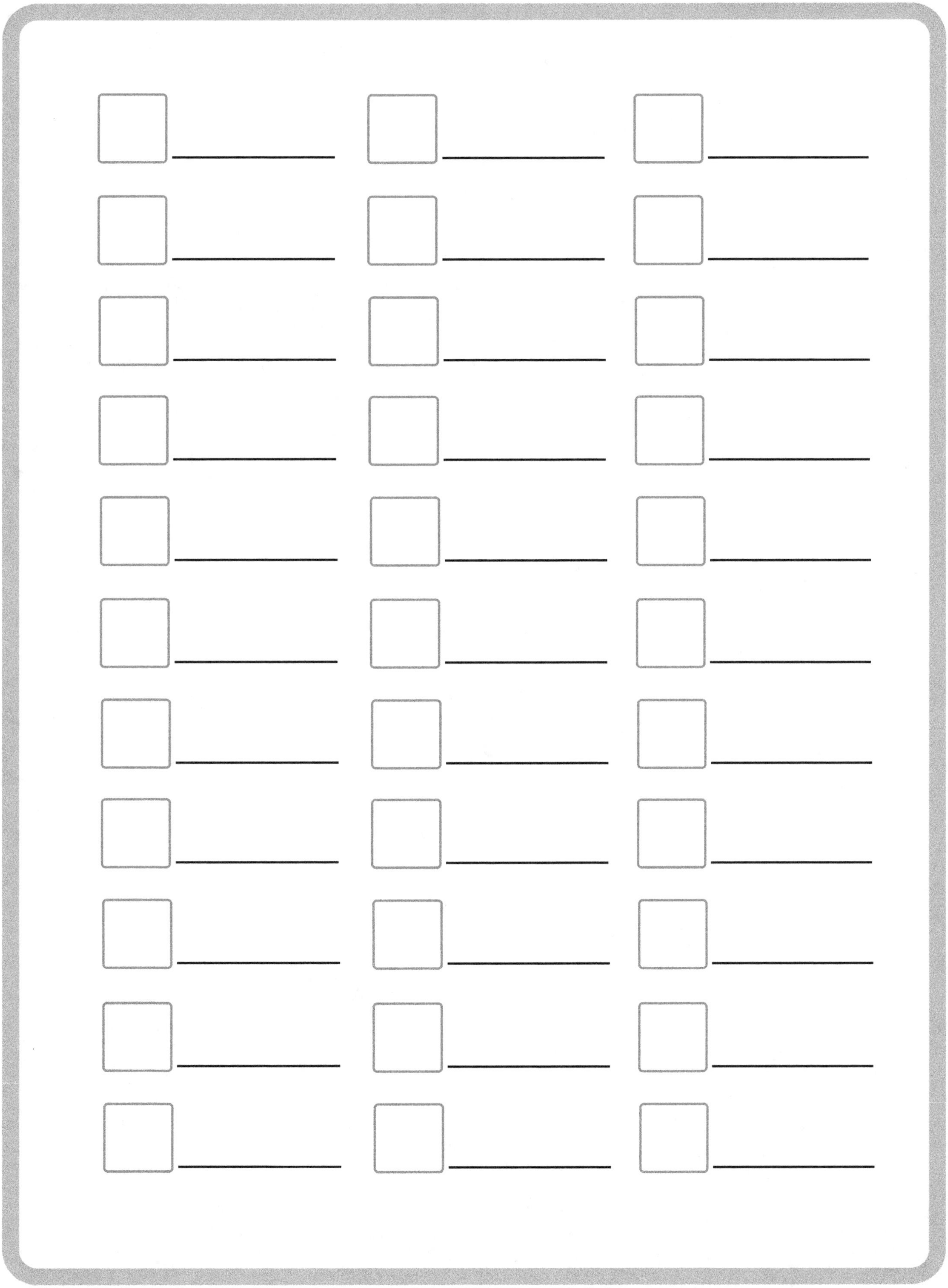

Solution

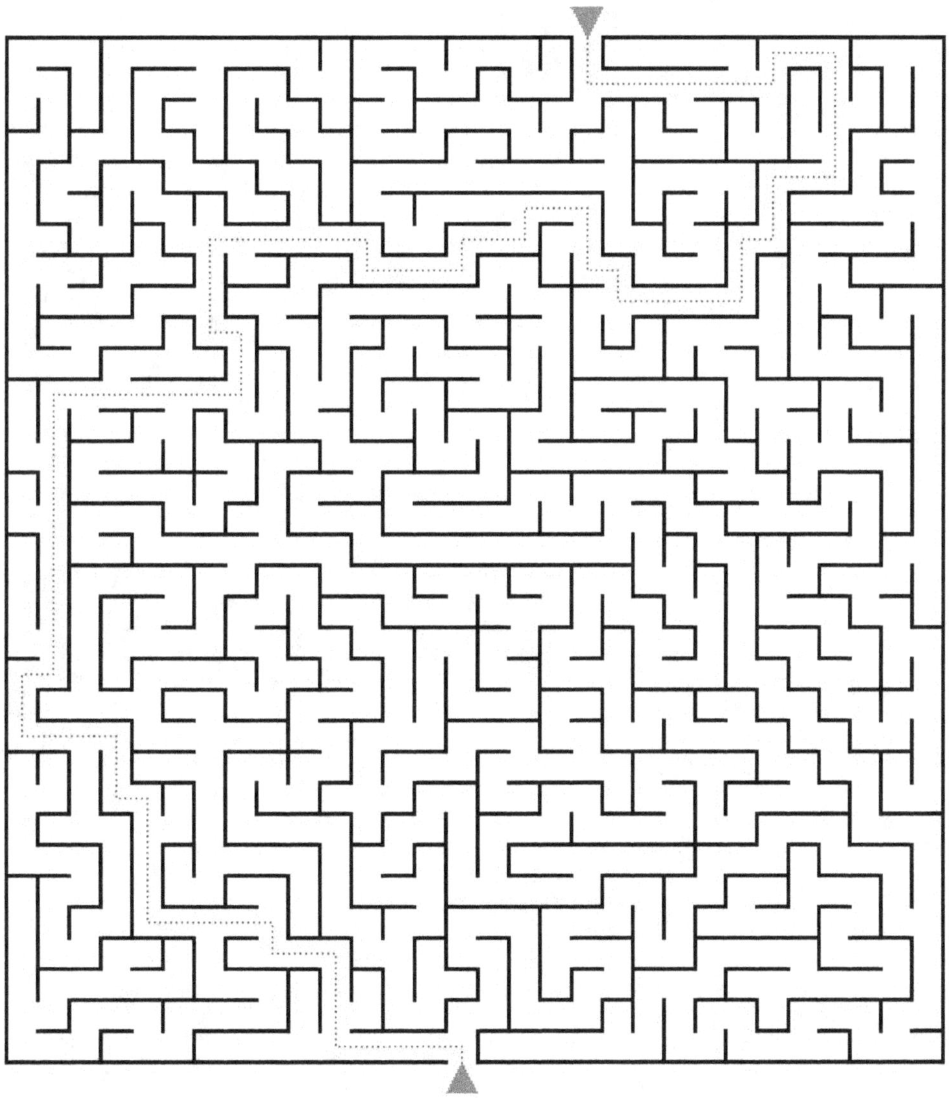

www.ingramcontent.com/pod-product-compliance
Lightning Source LLC
Chambersburg PA
CBHW081453220526
45466CB00008B/2624
9781691712472